Adolf Hitler

Learn How a Corporal Raised to Full Power

(A Comprehensive Biography of One of the Most Feared Leaders)

Stacey Fischer

Published By **Phil Dawson**

Stacey Fischer

All Rights Reserved

Adolf Hitler: Learn How a Corporal Raised to Full Power (A Comprehensive Biography of One of the Most Feared Leaders)

ISBN   978-1-77485-617-8

No part of this guidebook shall be reproduced in any form without permission in writing from the publisher except in the case of brief quotations embodied in critical articles or reviews.

Legal & Disclaimer

The information contained in this ebook is not designed to replace or take the place of any form of medicine or professional medical advice. The information in this ebook has been provided for educational & entertainment purposes only.

The information contained in this book has been compiled from sources deemed reliable, and it is accurate to the best of the Author's knowledge; however, the Author cannot guarantee its accuracy and validity and cannot be held liable for any errors or omissions. Changes are periodically made to this book. You must consult your doctor or get professional medical advice before using any of the suggested remedies, techniques, or information in this book.

Upon using the information contained in this book, you agree to hold harmless the Author from and against any damages, costs, and expenses, including any legal fees potentially resulting from the application of any of the information provided by this guide. This disclaimer applies to any damages or injury caused by the use and application, whether directly or indirectly, of any advice or information presented, whether for breach of contract, tort, negligence, personal injury, criminal intent, or under any other cause of action.

You agree to accept all risks of using the information presented inside this book. You need to consult a professional medical practitioner in order to ensure you are both able and healthy enough to participate in this program.

Table of Contents

Introduction 1

Chapter 1: Of Hitler's Childhood And Youth 5

Chapter 2: World War I Decorated Soldier 19

Chapter 3: A Young And Ambitious Politician 25

Chapter 4: Pursuit Of Power 37

Chapter 5: The Chancellor Of A Weak Germany 55

Chapter 6: Building The Power Of Military 68

Chapter 7: The Leader Of A War Machine 81

Chapter 8: After The War 104

Chapter 9: Path To Ruin 172

Introduction

It is believed that "The sleeping of the reasons creates creatures" This quote appears to be very relevant to the 20th century, a time which the economic downturn and crisis resulted in massive conflicts such as World War I and World War II. These are times that are conducive to the growth of radical groups because , when large numbers of people suffer from the effects of unemployment, poverty and other social catastrophes extreme movements are developing and, in some instances they are able to take over the power in these affected nations. The final days of World War I was the time for radical changes as the ancient empires that had ruled for centuries fell apart due to the pressures of the specific ethnic groups that helped to create these empires. In the end, the Russian Empire ended up being destroyed due to the development of Bolshevism as the Austrian Empire fell and eleven other nations rose from the ashes. It appeared that the German ethnic groups were the first to be afflicted since the end of the war brought harsh sanctions against them and certain of them were incorporated into other nations such as Poland as well as Czechoslovakia. The German population was looking for a leader who could rectify the injustices that were committed against them by Allies and to punish those who lied to them by signing the ceasefire armistice as well as the Treaty of Versailles. It turned out that the leader they were looking for wasn't even the name of a German citizen. In reality it had been an Austrian who had moved into Bavaria (Munich).

Adolf Hitler was a character who emerged from a disorganized and weak Germany He was a hero to many Germans believed that he was the one to save the nation out of its devastation and lead it towards fame and glory. Growing up in the midst of turmoil in society and being subjected to racist and anti-Semitic speech, he developed lots of hatred for Jews as well as the other Slavic nations. Being an Austrian citizen, he was embarrassed to be a member of a state that was multi-ethnic, where the German ethnic groups were marginalized compared to Slavic ethnic groups and even Jews. He was adamant about the Austrian social policies and eventually came to dislike Vienna due to its diverse ethnicity. The time he spent in Vienna was one of starvation and poverty lived a traditional living and was unable to improve his social standing as well as to earn an income that was steady. He was simply a dreamerwho was extremely enthusiastic about German culture and Wagner's operettas that would influence his views of German ultranationalism.

Vienna was never a city that he could call home, however, he was able to see Munich as a place where he was a part of as a genuine German city. In Munich, he honed his speaking skills. He was an advocate for a small right-wing group that was anti-Marxist, nationalist and anti-Semitic views. His message began to be heard by more people since his speeches made sense to larger viewers. He became the most influential figure in the Nazi party as he forced his ideas on others. It was the Beer Hall Putsch was a defeat for his political career however, it provided him with the chance to think and come up with better strategies to gain the power. In the time he was being in jail, he wrote his beliefs and thoughts into a book that was used as a political manifesto to The Nazi party. Following the release of his prisoners, he re-established the party to make it more powerful than ever before and was waiting for the right moment to take the power. According to some, Hitler employed democracy to end democracy in itself. This means that he had gained power through democratic means and, once in control, he declared himself the Fuhrer who seized all power in his own hands. The German people began to admire as well as fear Hitler, since they saw that the strength of Germany rising and the nation returned to its previous splendor. But, the power of too much was also a draw for enemies, either in or out of Germany and also made him appear more egocentric, since he was the one accountable of that German Army defeats on the battlefield. The losses were too serious to be able to recover from The allied forces were taking back the land that was occupied from the Germans.

All things come to an end, and Hitler's hopes and goals were shattered and completely destroyed by the wreckage of Berlin. In a period that was dominated by famous political figures such as Churchill as well as Roosevelt, Hitler is considered to be the most negative figure of the period (and possibly throughout the history of humanity) due to the fact that he is blamed for the loss of over twenty million civilians as well as soldiers.

Chapter 1: Of Hitler's Childhood And Youth

"I can remember the pale, gaunt youth very clearly. He was a gifted athlete but in a narrow field. He was also apathetic as he was known to be a bit cantankerous as well as arrogant, inconsiderate and irritable. He was not a great student and had trouble making friends at school. In addition the fact that He did not have the right attitude. lazy...his enthusiasm for work waned very quickly. He was averse to criticism or advice; in the same way, the other students to submit to their unqualified servitude and claimed to be as the head of the class ..." in the form of the Dr. Eduard Humer, one of Hitler's teachers.

A) Hitler's Origins

There were many theories pertaining to Hitler's birthplace, with some historians even claiming that the hated Nazi leader was of Jewish roots. The theory has never been confirmed, however, there's still an unanswered question about the birthplace of Hitler's father Alois Hitler Sr. He was the unlegitimate son of Maria Anna Schicklgruber. birthed in 1837. At this time, Alois was recognized as Schicklgruber. However, in 1842 Alois's mother got married to Johann Georg Hiedler, and Alois's father became Johann Georg Hiedler one who was officially registered with the name Georg Hitler. The Schicklgrubers were a modest family that was simple and poor from the northwestern portion in Lower Austria.

Alois was the very first affluent member of the family, one who aspired to climb in the ranks of society. When he was a young man Alois had a job in a mediocre post within the Austrian Ministry of Finance, however, despite his poor background and lack of education, he did manage to be promoted to higher levels. Thus, he was granted supervisor status in 1861and later a position in the customs service in 1864. In 1870, he was promoted to the position of a customs officer before moving in Braunau am Inn the next year, and was an inspector for customs in

1875. Being a social climber Alois might have taken on the name Hitler instead of Schicklgruber as it was simple and appealing. Also, beginning with the Final Authorization of 1877 he always was signed Alois Hitler. Alois got married to his future spouse (Klara Polzl) prior to having an remarkable career. After their name changed, the couple were second cousins. Klara Polizl was the eldest remaining daughter of Johanna's Huttler and Johann Baptist Polzl, a small-scale holder from Spital. But it was Klara's grandpa, Johann Nepomuk Huttler, the brother of Johann Georg Hiedler, who adopted Alois following the death of his brother. in death. The reason for this is that their relationship with their families is explained. When Klara was just sixteen years old she left the farm owned by her family in Spital to be a housekeeper at the house of Alois Hitler in Braunau am Inn.

Even though he was a star in his career, his personal life of Alois weren't in order. He was married three times. The first time , he was married to an older woman named Anna Glasserl, but the marriage was ended in 1880. In the second marriage, he was married to a very young woman, Franziska Matzelberger, but she died from tuberculosis at the age of just 23. When his second wife passed away in August 1884 Alois was a father of nine however four of them perished in the early years of their lives. In the two marriages he had, Klara wasn't a servant at the home of Alois. However, when Franziska was in a coma, she was moved to the surrounding area in Braunau am Inn. The children from the previous marriage were tiny and Alois was able to rely on Klara to look after his children who were young. Shortly after Franziska was killed, Klara became pregnant, however, a marriage between two cousins from the same family wasn't possible, and they had to obtain the approval of the Church. The condition of Klara was becoming more apparent and clear, the blessing from the Church was granted at the end of 1884. Alois Hitler as well as Klara Polzl were officially married on the 7th of January, 1885. The first child born of the marriage passed away very young, living only between two and three years old. The first child called Gustav came into the world in May 1885 , and died in December of 1887. The second was Ida and, like Gustav was sick with diphtheria, and passed away at the beginning of January in 1888. Third child Otto who passed away only a few days of his birth.

On the 20th of April, 1889, around 6:30 in the evening, Adolf Hitler was born. It was the day before Easter, and the fourth son from Alois as well as Klara Hitler was born into the world. Additionally, he was also the first child from this union to not die until the beginning of the year. In addition to his brothers and sisters, who were from his father's second and first marriages, Adolf also had a brother named Edmund (born around 1894, and passed away around 1900) and an older sister named Paula born around 1896. Alois had a high income that could provide a comfortable middle class lifestyle to his Hitler family. But this doesn't necessarily mean the Hitlers were able to live permanently in Braunau am Inn town. In the fall of the year 1898 Alois purchased a home and a piece of land in Leonding which was a village located close to Linz likely for the better education for children. Linz was always considered in the eyes of Adolf Hitler as his home town. He always considered it to be one of the more "Germanic" town in the Austro-Hungarian Empire. It brought together eleven nationalities within one state. It was a great location to be raised and a young Adolf was able to enjoy his childhood with no worries, but the slumbering life was soon to come to an end.

B) Studies and Passions

Following the death of the older brother Edmund in 1900, and due to the fact that his older younger brother Alois junior was living a rebellious lifestyle away from his family, Alois senior's ambitions fell upon the shoulders of his father Adolf. So, he wished for Adolf to go to Realschule, a school that focused on modern subjects such as sciences and technical studies that could be a excellent starting point for further education. He did not like the humanistic study and thought they were not practical to develop a career. When Alois realized the fact that son Adolf was taking too much interest in drawing, he decided to steer him away from humanistic study and the lifestyle associated with them.

Secondary school was an absolute nightmare to Adolf Hitler, as he did not have the time to build relationships and establish friendships. He was required to travel each morning to Leonding in Germany to Linz and return, that took over an hour in his daily routine. He hated most of the classes, and his school performance was mediocre and poor.

Absolutely, nothing his father had been imagining. At that stage, he'd turned into an introvert and unsocial teenager. The relationship he shared between his dad was difficult, with Realschule was the beginning of the conflict with Adolf as well as his dad. This was also the time during which he hid in stories of heroic acts in the German past. He then became a passionate German nationalist, expressing hatred and contempt for and the Austrian Empire. In his early school years, Adolf was just like the majority of youngsters, happy and enthusiastic. However, when he entered the second year of secondary school, he changed into a shrewd and rebellious teenager, who seemed to have no meaning in his life. He was the exact opposite of what his father fought against and shunned.

Alois Hitler passed away on the 3rd of January 1903 and left his family an idyllic circumstance. This meant that the young Adolf could pursue his dreams and no one could interfere with his plans. Adolf continued to struggle with poor grades at school, and he tried convincing his mom to leave the school. The family relocated to Linz and then to Linz, however Adolf was dismissed from at the

Realschule at the time. He enjoyed a relaxed life without any goals with his mother, aunt Johanna and his younger sisters, Paula looking after his requirements. Adolf had the freedom to follow the art of life and the majority of his hobbies were related to writing poetry or painting. He dreamed of becoming an accomplished artist and even began taking piano lessons to try to be an accomplished musician. The Linz Opera was one of his favourite activities as the realization came that becoming an artist requires socializing with fellow art enthusiasts. It was during the Linz Opera that he first got himself with the works that was created by Richard Wagner, as these dramas told stories from the glorious and mythical Germanic time. It was there that he fell with Wagner's work. Wagner and would form the foundation for an entirely new philosophy.

The passion for the arts inspired him to convince his mother to fund his excursion to Vienna to look at the photographs of the Court Museum. He spent 2 weeks on a tour around Vienna, the Austrian capital, taking in the top tourist destinations. It was during this journey that he came up with the idea of going to an art school called the Viennese

Academy of Fine Art. The aunt of his, Johanna was even able to help finance Adolf's studies at the most prestigious arts school within the Austrian Empire. In this time that my mother's breast cancer was discovered however, even the condition of his mother could not persuade young Adolf to renounce his dream to attend at the Viennese Academy of Fine Arts. He went to Vienna in the beginning of September 2017. And just one month later, he was going through the admissions examination for admission to the school of art. There were 113 students all together, however only twenty-eight were accepted to the Viennese Academy of Fine Arts. Adolf Hitler was not accepted at this prestigious institution However, He demanded an explanation to the rector of the academy. He was informed that his talents were not appropriate for the art school. But, it might prove beneficial to architecture.

Adolf Hitler didn't want to reveal to anyone in his home town be aware of his demise However, an incredibly devastating loss forced Hitler to return to his home. His mother's health was deteriorating rapidly, even though the doctor in the family was paying particular care to the condition of her.

On the 21st December, 1907 Klara Hitler was killed, leaving behind a grieving family. Adolf was most likely the one who was to be the one most affected the passing of his mother in the sense that he lost the person who was the closest to him and for whom he felt the greatest affection. The tragic loss of his mother sparked determination of young Hitler and was he faced with the brutal reality. Hitler returned to Vienna for the third time , with the goal to become an architect.

C) The first Extremists Beliefs

On February 19, 1908 less than two months since his mother's death The young Adolf went to Vienna three times. His next goal was to be an architect since he had become conscious of his situation in society. The money that was saved following the death of his father was mostly used for the care of his mother. Adolf had no savings and had to earn to earn an income. But he did not gave up on his dream of becoming an outstanding artist, and he was living the as he did before in Vienna. Adolf Hitler lived in Vienna for the subsequent five years, but the years that followed marked the transition of an time. The huge European city was the site of cultural, political social, and ethnic tensions, each having an impact on a young, impressionable man moving from the small city in Linz to the magnificent Austrian capital. In this time that his experiences in Vienna will form the extreme convictions he'll later exhibit in his life.

Young Adolf was a recipient of a modest orphanage allowance, which was barely enough to cover his daily cost in Vienna. While he was struggling with the scourge of poverty and hunger but he did nothing to improve his situation because being tied to work was not something was something he could handle. A majority times, he was at the operas at Schonbrunn Palace, or within the heart in the center of Vienna (Ringstrasse). As a devoted architect He still took his time gazing at the architecture of Vienna. Another of his passions was opera and opera, with Richard Wagner as his favorite composer. Out of all the works by Wagner his favorite was Lohengrin. He thought it was the most enjoyable, since the play he watched ten times the musical. A close friend who was a friend of Hitler of Linz (August Kubizek) was with him in Vienna to study at the identical Viennese Academic of Fine Arts. As opposed to Hitler who was not a student, Kubizek managed to gain admission to this Academy to pursue a degree in music. Adolf Hitler preferred to paint for a living and that's how he came across Reinhold Hanisch. He was the artist who assisted him in selling his art.

At the start of the 20th century Vienna had become a multicultural city, yet it also was the center of ethnic, social as well as political tension. Adolf Hitler was exposed to the tensions of all kinds and was becoming acquainted with the racist discourse. In this time, he began to admire Karl Lueger and Georg Ritter von Schonerer Two German nationalists who had anti-Semitic views. His acquaintance who was from Linz, August Kubizek was convinced that Hitler was an anti-Semite just before departing Linz to Vienna however Reinhold Hanisch believed that it was it was only during his time in Vienna young Adolf began to form his anti-Semitic opinions. He believed he was required to relocate to a more Germanic city because there was nothing but hatred and disdain for the Jews from Vienna.

In 1913, he made the decision to change his plans and, after receiving the final part of the estate of his father He moved into Munich within Germany. He was offered the chance to be a part of in the Austro-Hungarian Army and was called to take medical tests. On February 5, 1914 Hitler went to Salzburg for the exams however, he was deemed insufficient to serve in the military. He was nevertheless not dissatisfied since he did not want to be a part of this army of other nationalities since he was later convinced that the mix of ethnic groups and races was the reason for the demise of the empire of Austria-Hungary. Adolf Hitler returned to Munich in the year 1939, where he remained until the start in World War I.

At the time, Munich was a vibrant city to which young Hitler felt that he was part of the. While he was awestruck by the architectural beauty of Vienna however, he was of the opinion that the German populace in and within the Austrian Empire was at risk due to the pro-slave policies of the authorities. Furthermore, Hitler considered Vienna a "Babylon of all races" and that the mix of these different cultures led to the destruction of German cultural heritage. In Munich the German was at home and the 15 months he was there prior to the onset of

World War I was probably the most joyful time in his entire life. He believed that everything he learned from Wagner's operas and everything he imagined about German life was happening directly in front of his eyes. With stunning architecture and a lively society, Munich seemed to be the perfect city for Hitler. It was a place where one could live in peace without having to work or observe the pulse of the city through the bars, the theaters, or the opera. This was the city was his home, the perfect spot for a passionate German nationalist (although the majority of his entire life in Austria until now).

Chapter 2: World War I Decorated Soldier

"I looked at the document with nervous hands. No words could ever describe the happiness I felt...Within just a few hours I was wearing the uniform, which I had no intention to take off for more than six years." -- Adolf Hitler, Mein Kampf p.147 (after receiving the response after submitting the request for King Ludwig the III of Bavaria to be a part of Bavaria's Bavarian army as a volunteer despite the fact that he was of Austrian citizenship)

an) Voluntary for the German Army

The outbreak of war provided the perfect opportunity to Adolf Hitler to prove himself as an ardent nationalist. He believed that the war was necessary for the survival of Germany and its the future. He was not hesitant to sign up as a volunteer for the Bavarian Army. Even Bavarian authorities recognized the fact that Hitler's registration was likely an error of the administrative system. As the man is an Austrian citizen, he could have been allowed to return to Austria. He was permitted to serve within the

Bavarian Reserve Infantry Regiment 16 as a dispatcher, in charge of delivering messages to officers who were on the frontline. He was stationed in Fournes-en-Weppes where the headquarters of the regiment that was based in the Western Front in Belgium and France. Adolf Hitler was not in the trenches fighting with the enemies, but he was spending much of the war either on the frontline or just from it.

His official name within his position in the Bavarian Army as a Meldeganger as he was the soldier accountable for transferring messages between the Regiment's headquarters and the Company. Following the First Battle of Ypres, from October to November 1914 Adolf Hitler was promoted to the rank of corporal, also known as Gefreiter in German terminology. While he had aspirations of becoming an uncommissioned officers or Unteroffizier but this was his final promotion during World War I.

B) Battles and Decorations

Hitler was well-aware of the terrors that war brought during his service in the Western Front. As a dispatcher, the man had ample time to indulge in artistic pursuits and draw instructions and cartoons to be published in the newspaper of the army. Like most dispatch runners, he was not an easygoing person, so there were no acquaintances in the regiment he served in. He was, however, engaged enough on the frontline, and sent message during the First Battle of Ypres, the Battle of the Somme, the Battle of Arras and the Battle of Passchendaele. In the Battle of the Somme, one of the shells exploded in the dugout of runners and caused the young Gefreiter to sustain a laceration on his left leg. Following this tragic incident, he received to Beelitz Hospital in Beelitz and was there for more than two months. On March 5, 1917 Adolf Hitler returned to his regiment, and continued to send messages in the same way as prior to. On the 15th of October 1918, Adolf Hitler was sprayed by mustard gas, which resulted in temporary blindness. He was treated in the Pasewalk hospital, and there the doctor informed him about the German capitulation. After hearing about the news, he was suffering from temporary blindness for the second time.

His bravery and courage didn't get overlooked, as he was awarded some military awards throughout his time in the Western

Front. The year 1914 was the time he received an Iron Cross, second class and on August 4, 1918 his name was presented with an Iron Cross first class, on the advice of his Jewish lieutenant Hugo Gutmann. The Iron Cross is not usually awarded to Gefreiters. Gefreiter however Hitler convinced his superiors they were worthy of the distinction. He was also awarded the Black Wound Badge on May 18 1918. While the soldier was decorated, Adolf Hitler was not promoted to a position of superiority. His superior officers believed Hitler was not a leader with the required abilities. Additionally, being an introvert and having different nationality was an obstacle for him to be promoted to the rank of Underoffizier.

C) A) The Beginning of a New Ideology

Hitler believed that World War I as the most memorable of his experiences, however, that was not the only period in which his German nationalist sentiments were developed. When he was recuperating from the gas attack at the Pasewalk hospital when he learned of the surrender of Germany. He was shocked that an army , which did not defeat at the front would surrender its own forces to the enemies. The conclusion of World War I marked the period of time when empires crumbled under the pressure of the new nationalities. The Austro-Hungarian Empire was destroyed and so did that of the Ottoman as well as the German Empire. In the East the Russian Empire was destroyed by the influence of Bolshevism. The nations that Hitler hated won the war. Maps of Europe changed significantly and the German state was dealt a severe humiliation.

Hitler was, like many German patriotic citizens, felt that Germany was being sabotaged by politicians, Marxists, and Jews as well as all those signing the arms deal agreement that put an end to the fighting. They were later referred to as "November criminals." But, the true drama for Germany began after the agreement of Versailles which was a humiliating and unjust peace accord which was signed between Germany with all the Allied Powers. The treaty imposed severe economically-sanctioned Germany and also compensation costs that had that had to be collected. Additionally, Germany lost some territories and had to be demilitarized in areas in the Rhineland region. A majority of German patriots are in complete disagreement in Article 231 in the Treaty of Versailles, as it was believed to mean that Germany was the one responsible for the conflict.

The hatred towards Jews and Marxists the hatred that Hitler thought was responsible for the surrender of Germany, fuelled his political ambitions, and would determine his political direction from that point on. It was the Dolchstosslegende or the myth of the stab-in-the-back was the basis of his political career. He believed that the German people were being mistreated by the politicians, and he felt that someone was needed to step in and lift Germany from the ruin.

Chapter 3: A Young And Ambitious Politician

"The force that sets the historical torrents of religious and political movements is the force of speech. The vast majority of a populace are more susceptible to the persuasive power of the spoken word than the appeal of any other power." -- Adolf Hitler, Mein Kampf page. 100.

a) A New Voice for the Deutsche Arbeiterpartei

Following the conflict, Hitler went back to Munich after the war, only to find Munich, the place he adored and considered home changed. The period of transition following the war was extremely turbulent, particularly in the political sphere. Bavaria was run under the revolutionary Bavarian administration, who functioned as an National Council. The institution was governed by radical political parties, such as that of Social Democrats or the Independent Social Democrats. The chief of the state, Kurt Eisner, a radical Jew was murdered in 1919's spring and caused chaos in the Bavarian political scene. Then, in April Munich fell to communists, who saw Moscow as a model of political leadership. Munich had to be liberated from Soviet rule. This task was executed with the help of Reichswehr soldiers (army) as well as Freikorps (volunteers). Hitler was not a novice to the activities of the anti-revolutionary movement and was a participant in the process. At the age of thirty, he had no idea what was going on. old, he had no qualifications or knowledge, and thus having no future career opportunities He decided to remain as a soldier. The experience he gained in the field helped to secure a job as an intelligence officer in Munich.

Thus, he was given an assignment to join those of the tiny political party known as Deutsche Workers' Party, or Deutsche Arbeiterpartei (DAP). In recognition of his speaking skills and his leadership within the army believed to see him become an activist of the populist type (while still employed in the army) within this tiny group that they considered to be radical. Since much of the political discussion was discussed in the beer halls, Hitler was present at public debates in these spaces. He was known for his oratory abilities and during the DAP gathering on the 12th 1919, he was able to get the attention of the party's chairman, Anton Drexler. Hitler received a copy My Political Awakening, which is a manifesto of the political right that contained anti-capitalism and anti-Marxism ideas, and , in particular, anti-Semitic views. In the wake of his superiors in the army, Hitler joined the DAP and was a member of the party number 555 (apparently the DAP began with a count of members as five hundred so that it appeared they were a bigger party).

A few days later, Hitler had written his first written statement regarding his fellow Jews with his Gemlich letter. He wrote that the government's aim should be the elimination from all Jews. Then, Hitler was starting to feel more valued and important because his speeches were able to reach increasing numbers of people. The most prominent DAP party members DAP included Dietrich Eckart, who was one of the founding members. He was also an active participant in the Thule Society which is an organization that was occult. Eckart was able to take Hitler into his arms, and later became his mentor. Then, he introduced Hitler to Munich's upper class. Due to Eckart as well as Hitler working together with Hitler, the DAP began to become more well-known.

B) The birth of the Nazi Party

The year 1920 marked the birth of the Nazionalsozialistische Deutsche Arbeiterpartei NSDAP (National Socialist German Working Party). Hitler was the one who drew the logo of the party, which was a swirl of a swastika inside the white circle, and on an red background. In this moment it was clear that he was not a political agitator. Therefore, his discharge was granted by the army and was forced to work full-time with his Nazi party. With the assistance by Dietrich Eckart, Hitler became an even more effective speaker, with the ability to manipulate massive crowds. Its headquarters for the Nazi party was located in Munich which at the period became considered to be the "wasps nest" for anti-Marxists as well as anti-government German nationalists. Their primary aim was to eliminate Marxism and to abolish their own Weimar Republic. In February 1921, Hitler had already become a master of the podium who delivered a speech with the support of over 6000. Before the event some supporters of the party were scattered throughout Munich dispensing brochures and waved the swastika. The crowd was just captivated by the energy of Hitler, but equally impressed by his harsh words against political rivals, Treaty of Versailles, but mostly Marxists in general and Jews.

A larger party was not an unison party. Many friends of the party didn't acknowledge Hitler as the leader. Certain of the top members of the party wanted to join together with The German Socialist Party, but at the time, Hitler resigned from the party. They realized that, without Hitler the Nazi party would lose its most well-known and well-known public persona. The only requirement for a return was to replace Anton Drexler as party chairman. These leaders agreed, and Hitler joined in the Nazi Party as member 3680 on the 26th of July. There were still a few opposition members in the party who circulated a pamphlet that described Hitler as an apostate. But at the congress of the party on the 29th of July the party elected him chairman, 533 times and one against, and replaced Anton Drexler.

The party members were all over at the bar areas in Munich in which were numerous speeches delivered by Hitler. The message he delivered in his speeches was clear and it was a message that reached out to many people. The enthusiasm and gestures, as well as the voice all played into the hypnotic impact of his speech. He was averse to popular themes, focusing on the leaders who caused the financial crisis as well as his stance, the Treaty of Versailles, and the ways in which Jews and Marxists contributed to the suffering of Germany. In the era of his time it was this kind of speech that captivated the crowd.

Following the formation of the Nazi party the party's political agenda was made public. It contained 25 points, which is why it cannot be considered to be an ideology of a political party since it doesn't have the coherence to it. The Pan-Germanic movement was the inspiration for these ideas and included a few elements, such as opposing The Treaty of Versailles, some socialist ideas, anti-capitalism, antisemitism, and ultranationalism. The program was also thought of as to be a method of propaganda and proved highly effective in recruiting new members.

The most influential Nazi members included Rudolf Hess, Hermann Goring as well as Ernst Rohm. The latter was given the responsibility of creating the SA (Stormtroopers) as the Nazi Party feared paramilitary organization that was responsible for securing gatherings and threatening opposition politicians. At this point the party was expanding in size and attracting not just new members but new sponsors. Hitler's hatred for Jews was further exacerbated due to the influence on the Aufbau Vereinigung had on him. This was a conspiracy-minded organization of Russians who were against the Bolsheviks and believed that there was an Jewish conspiracy to explain the development of Bolshevism because the Jewish international financial system was linked with the movement.

C) the Beer Hall Putsch

1919 was a period of political instability in Munich and was ended with the Reichswehr intervention along with the Freikorps A couple of years later tensions escalated because people were not able to agree with the cruel measures made in the Treaty of Versailles. It was clear that the Republic of Weimar was too fragile to manage these tensions and during times similar to those, radical ideas were circulating in the minds. In Munich there was a feeling that there was a feeling that the Nazi Party felt like the communists were seeking to take control, so Hitler considered that this was the best time to strike. Even though the entire country was united under an unifying force, the French occupation of the Ruhr area since 1923's beginning however, the authorities in Berlin believed that passive resistance was sufficient in this scenario.

In the year 2000, the Nazi party stepped up its activities and was able to increase its presence with Hitler making more speeches in the beer halls. The aim of the party currently is to take control over Munich and then march into Berlin to try to take the power. Hitler was influenced by the work of Benito Mussolini's "March on Rome" which was a coup d'état initiated within Italy through "Il Duce" that was successful, and he was appointed the premier. Hitler believed that it was the best time to take action, even though his party was unpopular outside Bavaria. He planned to take control of Munich as well as Bavaria and then marching on Berlin to protest against the ruling party. To gain control of Munich it would be necessary to have the support of three crucial individuals in Munich three key figures: the state commissioner Gustav Ritter von Kahr, the Chief of Police Hans Ritter von Seisser and the Reichswehr General Otto von Lossow. Kahr was already in the position of having almost dictatorial authority over Bavaria and had recently been able to ban most public gatherings of any political party in fear of a coup by the Left-wing or right-wing extremists.

After his return from exile to Sweden, Erich von Ludendorff was an army general who was a legend among Germans who did not lose an engagement in World War I, but was denigrated by the political leaders in"the "home battlefield." Hitler knew that to accomplish his goals Ludendorff was the one to support his cause because he was an admired figure among the officers of the army and within the political elite from the Bavarian Government. In 1923, Hitler managed to get Ludendorff on his side, and at the time he was attempting to gain support from the three individuals who held the monopoly power in Bavaria. Looking for the right moment and a way to gain support, the Nazis discovered they had a public gathering on November 8th, 1923, at the Burgerbraukeller brewery where three of the key individuals were in attendance. Hitler and a few Nazi members and the SA entered the bar and interrupted Kahr's speech before 3000 people. They announced the start of a national revolution and announcing the creation of a new government , with General Erich von Ludendorff as the important leader. Hitler requested assistance from Kahr Seisser, Kahr Lossow and received it. The Nazi members were able to seize their local offices of the Reichswehr as well as the Police. The following day Hitler along with his Nazi followers were planning to walk from Beer Hall to Bavarian War Ministry, in his plan to take over the Bavarian government. However, Kahr Seisser, Kahr and Lossow quit their support, meaning neither the police or the army joined forces with Hitler's troops. Instead the Nazi members as well as the SA were repelled by the police as they attempted to take power back in Bavaria. 16 members of Nazi group members died during the attempt, and four police officers were killed from the gunshots.

Hitler was able to escape, and flew away to Ernst Hanfstaengl's home where he was hiding. A few days later on the 11th of November 1923, Hitler was convicted for high in treason. The trial started with the People's Court and on April 1st, 1924 Hitler got his five-year sentence' imprisonment at Landsberg Prison. It was during this time that the Nazi Party was left in the control by Alfred Rosenberg, who acted as the interim leader. It was while in prison that Rosenberg composed Mein Kampf, a book that contained all anti-Semitic and anti-Marxist beliefs he held. The book portrays Jews as a scourge and "international toxic agents" of the society. According to the book the only way to get rid of them was to eliminate the Jews However, the book made no reference to this process and what it is made up of. Between 1925 until 1932, Mein Kampf was sold in over 228 thousand copies. Between 1932 and 1933 the book was sold out in 1 million copies. He was not treated badly within Landsberg Prison as he received an individualized and friendly treatment from guards, along with letters and visits from other Nazi members, including his deputy Rudolf Hess.

On the 20th of December 1924 Hitler got his release from Landsberg prison following a period of just nine months there. It was the Bavarian Supreme Court pardoned him and, despite the opposition of the state prosecutor

Hitler was released and more determined than ever to gain power and influence over Germany. But this time, Hitler would think more carefully prior to attempting to gain power, as his decision to take over the Beer Hall Putsch was more than an instinctive response and a "now or never" circumstance in which he felt it was the best moment to take action. This was not the outcome of a meticulous plan but Hitler could have a moment to reflect while in prison over the reasons for what was wrong. Instead of being a frenzied leader like the Nazis did prior to the unsuccessful election, Hitler would dedicate his time in order to build and organize the Nazi party to be the most powerful political power in Germany.

The Bavarian government sought to exile Hitler from Austria since they were they cognizant of the administrative mistake which was committed by allowing Hitler to be a part of in the Bavarian Reserve Regiment in World War I. But the request was turned down from the Austrian federal chancellor who claimed that the service with the German Army made Hitler's Austrian citizenship null and void. On April 7th, 1925 Hitler declared his Austrian citizenship, since he was working to rebuild his Nazi party.

Chapter 4: Pursuit Of Power

"I am able to look back to the moment when , along with six other unidentified people I established this organization in the year 2000, and I was able to address eleven twelve thirteen fourteen, twenty thirty fifty, and thirty. If I think back to how, I gained sixty-four members to the cause, I am forced to admit that the movement that is happening today with a flow of millions of people are joining our organization, is that is unique to German history. The bourgeois parties had 70 years of work to do. Where is the group that over the course of seventy years has managed to achieve the same things we've achieved in just twelve years?" - Adolf Hitler's speech at the Industry Club in Dusseldorf, 27 January 1932.

A) The Years Following the Prison Release

The effects that resulted from the Beer Hall Putsch were catastrophic for the Nazi Party, as the party was effectively banned across Bavaria. At the time of Hitler's exile the political scene had become less tense and the economy had increased, which meant there was less opportunity for the agitations of Hitler's political party. The party was not only outlawed, but their presence in the media, including the publication Volkischer Beobacher was also prohibited. Certain Nazi party's leaders fled to other countries (Hermann Goring returned only in 1927) and others were killed by shots fired during the putsch or passed away shortly afterward. Hitler's mentor Dietrich Eckart died at the end of 1923, and the party was without leaders during this time. Hitler chose Alfred Rosenberg to handle the party's affairs, but his party had been banned as a result of the putsch that failed. Rosenberg wasn't a leader therefore Hitler considered that his place within the party wasn't in danger by Rosenberg because Rosenberg was not an agent of the action and was unable to give any power.

In the time of Hitler's imprisonment There was a conflict with Rosenberg as well as the radical wing of the party, represented through Julius Streicher and Hermann Esser. Adolf Hitler didn't want the party to be able to thrive without him, which is why he did not choose one side of this battle. Leaders such as Rosenberg Ludendorff, Strasser, or Rohm were determined to take part in the national and state elections in the spring of 1924. In the spring of 1924, Hitler was in a state of rage over radical ideas that led to the publication the novel Mein Kampf, so he opposed any parliamentary or democratic activity. He was concerned about his standing within the party , if other party leaders were elected in the Reichstag. Since the party was not a part of laws, Nazi leaders could get candidates by means of Volkisch group. (people's groups). The leaders like Rosenberg Ludendorff, Strasser, Feder, Rohm and Frick made it onto their list for the National Socialist German Freedom Movement that was an unimportant people's group within those in the Volkisch group, and eventually became the second-largest political power within the Reichstag. The Nazis had the chance to win 32 seats within the German Parliament (Reichstag), which was a modest success in the elections held between March and April 1924. Hitler was not entirely convinced about the outcome, but for Strasser and Ludendorff, it was a way to build on the alliance that between the Nazis of Bavaria formed together with North German Deutsch-volkische Freitheitspartei, the radical party of Northern Germany, led by Albrecht of Graefe along with Graf Ernst zu Reventlow, who held the same extreme opinions like they did the Bavarian Nazis (ultranationalist and anti-Semitic, racist and anti-Racist views). Hitler was opposed to any form of alliance as the alliances could affect the goal and strength of the party. Additionally, he was concerned about his position within the party, since the Nazi leaders didn't think about his position. He was a fan of a small-sized group, but a pure one and easy to manage. The film Mein Kampf, Hitler was convinced that the strongest is the strongest when it's on its own.

Another reason for the frustration of Hitler had to do with the early release from Ernst Rohm, who quickly began to build the Frontbann Stormtroopers on the scale of. The group grew rapidly and had thousands of new recruits across various regions which included East Prussia and Austria. The SA was initially designed for intimidation of political enemies as well as to spread propaganda. However, although it was well-organized, it began to become difficult to keep under control. Hitler believed that Rohm's actions Rohm could delay his release from prison.

When the economy began to recover and elections were held for the Reichstag The votes for the Nazi people's bloc plummeted significantly and there were only fourteen Nazi politicians got seats in the parliament. Hitler was able to avoid deportation to Austria during his time in prison, which meant that it was his turn to rebuild the party. Certain leaders such as Rosenberg Ludendorff, Ludendorff and Rohm became disgraced and Hitler was determined to restore the party and expand the propaganda activities. Two months after his release, Volksicher Beobachter appeared again, having a consistent editorial that was signed by Hitler. However, the Nazis weren't quite ready to let him run the party. It was not until after his address on the 27th of February 1925 in the Burgerbraukeller beer hall in Berlin, that the remaining Nazi supporters accepted him as their rightful leader. This marked the rebirth of the Nazi Party and with it Hitler had two primary goals: to eliminate any opponent that was a part of the party as well as to establish an effective political organization within the legal rules. Similar to the Phoenix that was the Phoenix, the Nazi party had emerged from the ashes of its former self. In the same location that was the site of its defeat and ban it was reinstated.

The 1925 Presidential elections were a complete fail to the Nazi party, since their candidate Erich von Ludendorff only obtained only 211 thousand votes of 27 million. Then, Hitler realized that Ludendorff wasn't a good fit to him, and so his former World War I general fell into the abyss. At this moment the Nazis had a strong support for Field-Marshal of Hindenburg as a last-minute presidential candidate that was backed by the nationalists, who were defeated by a small margin. The economy was still in recovery and Hitler's ideas were not popular with Germany's Nationalists. As he was not a fan of alliances with other political parties, Hitler trusted Joseph Goebbels as well as his fellow Strasser brothers (Gregor and Otto) to build and grow the party in northern Germany. But the odds were not in favor of the political goals of Hitler because the money to the group was difficult to obtain and in the parliamentary elections in 1928 the party was only able to get 2.6 percent of votes, which was a total of 810100 votes. Hitler's speeches did not appeal to the massive crowds, because the people didn't find themselves in this adolescent rhetoric. However it was the Nazis tried to be more prominent in social life by organising parties however they didn't gain any popularity.

But, the fortunes of Hitler were going to change due to the decline of the global economy. In 1929, the Crash of 1929 was the ideal opportunity to allow Hitler and his gang to ascend to the heights of power. Germany was badly affected by the crisis since unemployment rose to the extreme, with more than six million Germans are now suffering from this situation. The financial system collapsed and the people's money and savings were at risk. Hitler offered a solution to the person responsible and repeated it in his numerous speeches. But, they also offered solutions to the crisis such as boosting the economy, creating jobs for the jobless and breaching the Treaty of Versailles. With these famous topics and powerful speeches, the Nazis could rise to power. The elections in

September 1930 enabled the party to be a important political force within the Reichstag.

(b) A) The Nazi Party Becomes a Power within the Reichstag

The Great Depression was the perfect chance for extremists to become popular , and sometimes to be able to rule the country. It was also that the Nazis received the greatest support. They were the Strasser brothers were successful in building the party in northern of Germany However, Hitler established new relationships with people like Otto Dietrich, who owned an all-encompassing press agency. Hitler's speeches were being broadcast all over the world and he was gaining recognition throughout Germany. In the past the only place he was known was in Bavaria however, Germans from other regions had no idea about the man. Otto Dietrich was the son-in-law of the political advisers of the Mining Union in the Ruhr area and the owner of Rheinisch-Westfalische Zeitung, the newspaper of the Ruhr area industrialists. This is how Hitler came into contact with Emil Kirdorf, one of the most famous names of that German industry. He was the one in charge of all the money for the Mining Union.

Hitler was able to raise funding for his party and his plans to take over the ruling party had an opportunity to succeed. His ideas and speeches would now be heard by a larger audience. He also managed to get his supporters involved in celebrations , and even fundraising events. They also provided entertainment and food for thousands of Germans. The efforts of the Germans weren't in vain, as the result was to be seen in the elections to the Reichstag in September 1930. The Nazi party garnered over 6.4 millions votes which is 18.3 percent of all votes. The elections dealt a huge blow to the center-right parties, since the Nazis won 107 seats on the Reichstag (making them the second major force in Germany) along with other extremist parties also won significant numbers of members within the German Parliament. Hindenburg as the president elected did not want to hand the power over to extreme parties. So the minority cabinet was put in place with the role of a puppet chancellor, Heinrich Bruning from the Centre Party. This Bruning administration was merely an easier phase of the dictatorship since the chancellor was running the government through emergency decrees directly by the President. This administration was therefore required to implement austerity measures as Germans were losing their jobs. In fact, the majority of the inflation was impacting the entire population of Germany.

It was nearly seven years after Hitler abdicated his Austrian citizenship before he was granted his German citizenship granted to him by Dietrich Klagges, who was an active part of the Nazi party, and also the minister of the interior in Brunswick. On February 25 1932 Hitler received his official recognition as an official citizen of Brunswick and was subsequently an official German citizen. It was the perfect time because Hitler was running for president against the independent candidate Paul von Hindenburg, the currently the President of Germany. Although Hitler was runner-up in both occasions, (on March 13 and April 10 1932) his loss was compensated by the enormous performance in the Nazi party during the Reichstag elections in July 1932. The party received 37.3 per cent of votes with a minimum of 13.74 millions of votes. Thus, the Nazi party now had more than 230 seats in the German

Parliament. The parties of the center were in decline, since these austerity policies had grave implications for a large portion of the German populace. Paul von Hindenburg's principal opponents in his campaign included Hitler as well as Ernst Thalmann (the leader of the KPD which was known as the German Communist Party). The Reichstag elections, the majority members were won by extremist groups, even when Hindenburg requested a new election for the parliamentary system in November 1932, one month after the Hitler's massive victory in the previous election. Hindenburg's hopes of the formation of a majority government quickly faded due to the results of Reichstag elections. Although it lost a couple of seats in the parliament however, the Nazi party was still the largest power in politics, holding the majority of 196 seats.

Hitler was backed by German industrialists who believed in him the only able person to restore Germany to its previous glory. Many of the most powerful politicians such as Franz von Papen and Alfred Hugenberg were also in support of Hitler and sent a letter Hindenburg seeking to convince Hindenburg to name Hitler as the Chancellor of Germany. Hindenburg was adamant about this idea and on the 30th of January 1933, announced Hitler as his new chancellor The cabinet was constituted by just three Nazi members: Adolf Hitler (chancellor), Wilhelm Frick (Minister of the Interior) and Hermann Goring, who was named Secretary of the Interior in Prussia. Hitler was granted what he desired, the chancellor's position as well as the supervision of the police across Germany.

C) The fall of Weimar Republic

The Weimar Republic, a form of government created to restore order and help guide Germany through the difficult times to follow, was the consequence of the Kaiser's demise on November 18, 1918. The politicians were required to implement the terms from the Treaty of Versailles, including the deportation of territories, the imposing of economic sanctions, and the demilitarization of the Rhine region. It was not an easy task since they had to contend with massive unemployment, hyperinflation and social unrest. The republic was home to two presidents who served for a longer time. The first included Friedrich Ebert, who acted as president from February 11, 1919 until February 28. 1925. The other of them was

Paul von Hindenburg, who was the president starting on May 12th, 1925 until August 2, 1934.

Although this kind of structure was a great way to organize the democratic process, which was in the hands of both the constitution and government, it was not without its drawbacks. The first was proportional representation, which meant that every party could receive the number of members in the Reichstag in proportion to the percentage of votes they received. That meant that every party that had a majority of votes (it was not important the number) could be able to gain seats in the Reichstag and consequently blocked laws. Furthermore, governments were extremely susceptible to this type of government, since they could fall on numerous occasions when there was not an overwhelming majority in the Reichstag to back the government. The other issue with The Weimar Republic is Article 48 which granted the president the power to rule in the event of an emergency, and the power to act without Reichstag approval. In the case of President Paul von Hindenburg used this option during his Bruning administration.

The extremists were a major threat to the Republic and there were attempts to topple an administration in a way that was not democratic. However, when the economic conditions in Germany was extremely bad and unemployment was extremely high both the right and left extreme political parties (the extremists) were able to gain a significant amount of votes and support. They rapidly began filling the seats in the Reichstag and made it difficult to pass laws, particularly those issued from parties like the Centre parties. In the Great Depression was the devastating attack on the Weimar Republic because it gave the political agitators a reason to prosper and to gain popularity from large crowds. Because they were ruled by the state authorities far too accommodating to the extremes, the communist as well as ultranationalist movement was growing in a huge way.

While German politicians collaborated with the politicians of the Allies in negotiating a deal on military debts Germany was still required to pay to the Allies and the majority of German nationalists were enraged by the amount of money that the country was required to pay as an apology to Allies. Some radical politicians even proposed the referendum that had intent of breaking the Treaty of Versailles and make an offence of the co-operation of German politicians in the pursuit of compensation. Even though the referendum was launched on the 22nd of December 1929, in the wake of the Young Plan, Germans were not very enthusiastic about voting on this issue, since only 15 per cent citizens who voted. The failed referendum only fueled Hitler's plans to gain the power to correct the injustices committed to Germany.

Participating in the election for President was a way to make Hitler be aware of the German people's attitude towards his views and ideas. The campaign he ran "Hitler over Deutschland" (Hitler over Germany) was a great success however he was defeated in the election to Paul von Hindenburg. In all likelihood, He was among the first politicians to utilize aircrafts for political reasons and was able to fly to the largest cities in Germany and seduce the crowd by his lively speeches. He was able to win nearly 37 percent of the votes, yet the Nazi party soon became the biggest name on the political stage of Germany.

The Reichstag elections in July and November 1932 demonstrated the Hindenburg his that Nazis were the most powerful political power in Germany and that there wasn't enough support from the Reichstag for the establishment of a central government. In the hands of Franz von Papen and Alfred Hugenberg both powerful politicians from that time, Hindenburg named Adolf Hitler as the chancellor of Germany. Hitler also secured two places in his cabinet for his party members. So, Wilhelm Frick was named the Minister of Interior as well as Hermann Goring was appointed Minister of Interior for Prussia. So, the Nazi party took over the police force in Germany.

Hitler set out to take over power meticulously, just as a skilled chess player. Upon being appointed chancellor, he destroyed his political foes. Gradually He gained power and gradually seized all the power Hindenburg was able to wield. 1933 was the year that Hitler began his dictatorship, however it wasn't until 1934 that he declared himself Fuhrer following the death of Hindenburg after it was announced that the Weimar Republic had officially ended.

Though it was intended to be an organization that was democratic However, the last times of the Weimar Republic were closer to the dictatorship of the past than to democracy. The power was centralized within the hands of Hindenburg, Papen and Schleicher and they received the support of the largest industrialists, estate-owners and the military. The lobbyists of all these groups are not interested in the same things, but they all were keen on destroying the constitution-based party system as well as the crushing on Marxism and the trade unions but they also had an interest in restoring a certain form of authoritarianism. This was the main goal among these groups of elites that were a part of a variety of parties. Because the election for Reichstag did not yield a conclusive outcome, since there was no party with an overwhelming majority, they were forced choose one of the most powerful political leaders to lead Germany towards an authoritarian government. The man they were searching for was Adolf Hitler, who now was a popular figure and was an icon that could not be ignored.

It is believed it was The Weimar Republic collapsed because of the repercussions caused by the Great Depression which were affecting Germany however, the gravestone of this regime was laid by lobby groups, who chose the right person to eliminate the system and bring the country into an autocratic government. At the time Hitler was appointed chancellor, The Weimar Republic was in a state of coma, and died simultaneously with its president.

Chapter 5: The Chancellor Of A Weak

Germany

"The fight is a relatively easy one as we can use every tool from the government. Radio and Press are at our available. We will create the greatest work of propagandism. The money will be there in this case." Joseph Goebbels

A) Rise to Power

Once Hitler was in power, he took all he could to strengthen his power, fighting his political adversaries to gain the majority of the Reichstag to back his government. Hitler needed to hold additional parliament elections to achieve this target. But something very unusual had to occur to trigger additional elections. In 1933, on February 27 the Reichstag building was burned in a fire that the Nazis blamed communists. Hitler was able to convince Hindenburg to take action in accordance with Article 48 and issue the Reichstag Fire Decree, a law that removed any rights and allowed detention with no trial. This provided the perfect opportunity to The SA (having over 2 million registered members) to target communist party members and to engage in violent anti-communist protests. All operations that were carried out by those of German Communist Party (KPD) were forbidden and more than 4000 KPD members were detained.

The date for the elections was March 6, 1933. This provided the Nazi party an excuse to ramp up the anti-communist campaign in the days prior to the elections. The campaign paid off since the Nazis received 43.9 percentage of votes, resulting with 288 members in the Reichstag. But it wasn't enough to create an overwhelming majority in the government, and the Nazis were forced to form a coalition with DNVP. The 21st of March, 1933 was the day of the brand new Reichstag that was celebrated by a formal opening ceremony in Potsdam. Because he was able to win the majority by forming one-sided alliances with different party Hitler did not intend to make use of the alliance because he was not a believer in any alliance with a different party. His cabinet instead issued the Enabling Act or Gesetz zur Behebung der Not von Volk und

Reich (or The Law to remedy the distress of the people and Reich) that granted Hitler the authority to make legislation for four consecutive years, without the acceptance by the Reichstag. This law was approved by in the Reichstag with 441 votes in support and 84 opposed In this way, Hitler was declared the leader of Germany.

He was in full control and, to consolidate it he began suppressing his political adversaries. "The "Iron Fist" of the Nazi party was responsible for threatening political leaders who did not support those who supported the Nazi party. Hitler knew that he needed to gain control of the working classes. So he disbanded all trade unions and detained all their leaders. The Nazis established their own German Labour Front, an organization that was created to represent business owners as well as administrators and employees.

Hitler also instructed his SA troops to terrorize the Nazis allies that is the DNVP and to convince the DNVP's chief (Alfred Hugenberg) to step down on June 29th the 29th of June, 1933. Assuring the safety of other opposition politicians, as well as friends, Hitler announced his belief that it was the

Nazi group was the sole legally-constituted official political organization in Germany (July 14th 13th, 1933). Within the party he was a member of, because there were still a few members who opposed his policies, he initiated an extermination in his own Nazi party. But, the process must be directed at the SA in addition, since he believed that it had grown into an organization that was difficult to manage, uncontrolled and that ate up huge resources. The troopers posed an affront to the political as well as military and industrial leaders. Hitler believed that the organization was a distraction from his main goal. It was necessary to take action, therefore Hitler planned murder of Ernst Rohm and other SA leaders, as well as other politicians, such as Gregor Strasser and Kurt von Schleicher. The purge was known as"the Night of the Long Knives and occurred from June 30 to June 2 until July 2nd the 2nd of July, 1934.

b) Fuhrer

On the 2nd of August on 1934, the demise of the President Hindenburg also marked the end of the Weimar Republic. But, just a day prior, Hitler issued the "Law regarding the highest State Office of the Reich," which stipulated the removal of the post of the president and the powers of the president with the powers for the chancellor. The law created Hitler the head of state and the Head of the government. He was officially referred to as Fuhrer and Reichskanzler however the latter title was quickly removed. At that point, no one in Germany could topple Hitler and he was the leader supreme of the country.

The shy Austrian who was without career perspective until the year 25 years ago, declared himself to be the Fuhrer of Germany in a position that was able to exercise all power in Germany at one time regardless of whether it was legislative, executive, or military. He was able to achieve this power in a step-by-step manner beginning by gaining popular support and then assuming the Reichstag and removing all opposition from in and outside the Nazi party, and taking advantage of a president that was easily manipulable. When he took office in the month of August, 1934 Hitler had the perfect opportunity to pursue his vision further and correct the injustice that was caused to Germany through the Treaty of Versailles and the Young Plan. His goal was to steer

Germany through the Great Depression and direct it towards a more prosperous and brighter future. It wasn't an easy job but the majority of Germans thought he was the ideal person to guide Germany in the right direction.

Since his early days as an agitator for political change, to the point that his rise to the position of the supreme leader of Germany He's changed considerably. At first his audience was just a small group in a bar however, he had developed into a master of performing live in the presence of hundreds of thousands. He was able to seduce people with his message and entice them to join an Nazi side. His message was straightforward and it was heard by thousands of Germans who believed his words. The humble background of Hitler (a commoner) was another factor that allowed him to reach the masses. When the German populace lost their faith in the ruling elite who was blamed for the disastrous consequences caused by the Treaty of Versailles, they wanted a savior to bring Germany back to glory. The German people believed that this person would have to be from within themselves since only one person can have the exact experience they were going through.

Although his admission to politics was somehow orchestrated by the military, because his purpose was to break into the radical political group, soon he found himself enjoying the task so much that was elected a full-time politician. Delivering speeches on the difficult times Germany was living in as well as about the traitors that brought this nation to its knees and he believed that he had discovered his real goal, which was to defend Germany from Marxists and Jews. After spending nine months in prison did he become an older politician, in contrast to before the Beer Hall Putsch he had the zeal of a young and affluent politician who was determined to bring himself to the top of the political ladder. The putsch's failure would be an utter blow to the Nazi party, since it were banned from the political scene for an short period and even though the party was reestablished in 1925, only after it's participation in the Great Depression did the party gain its popularity.

Following his release from prison, Hitler started consolidating his power within the

Nazi party. He established the foundations of a larger organised party that would with a presence all over Germany. The Nazi leader began using propaganda on an entirely different level and his message rang all Germans. Hitler also enlisted the party in community events in order to make people conscious of his party. He perfected his speech and at the time Germany was facing major economic problems people saw his speech to be the most sensible. The growing support of larger numbers of people, powerful industrialists and press agencies owners has transformed Hitler from an ordinary politician into an influential political figure all over the world. In the Great Depression helped the Nazi party gain power, since at the time Hitler began his campaign for president in 1932 the Nazi party was the most powerful political group across Germany. It assumed control of the Reichstag in a manner that was democratic and once it gained power, it was able to eliminate all the other parties. Hitler was appointed chancellor and he maintained his position until he became the dictator in fact of Germany. The death of the president Hindenburg resulted in the fact that the last legal factor that could exercise his power was no longer in place and he was able to take all authority within Germany in his own hands.

C) Consolidating Power

With complete power over Germany, Hitler started to carry out his plans for the German populace and to carry out the promises he made. This was at a time that the country was struggling with unemployment, so Hitler had come up with a method to offer jobs to the unemployed and those in need. The solution was to build of a huge autobahn, also known as Germans were known as, "Autobahn," which offered work to many. Hitler himself tried to show the way with video footages showing his working side-by-side with the German citizens to construct the autobahns. The motorways of today's Germany are a legacy of the time of Hitler. But they were not the only ones. Nazis weren't content with motorways. They also constructed dams, railways that covered a vast area as well as other works of civil engineering. While Hitler was preparing for war, he encouraged production of military weapons at the steel factories that were already in operation. These measures resulted in more jobs for

German population and, even though salaries were less than those from those of the Weimar Republic and an average German worked between forty-seven and fifty hours a week Hitler was able to manage the working class and stop any uprisings.

The Nazi propaganda was the mainstay of the media and every word that was broadcast on radio, as well as every piece published in the newspapers had to receive the approval of the Nazis. This was the way the regime promoted only its successes and kept from the public's view what was happening to the Jews and other groups that the Nazis were averse to. The swastika could be seen everywhere, and the official salute changed to "Heil Hitler!" that also included the gesture of lifting the right hand up into the air while straightening your hand.

Hitler would have liked to create an effective regime that could last for a thousand years. He was always convinced that the final legacy of such a system was its architecture. Since he was always enthusiastic with architecture, he stumbled upon an architect of the young age who shared his views and could implement Hitler's version of Classic German Culture.

Albert Speer was the architect who Hitler believed was capable of implementing his ideas. So he was given the task of the construction renovations in Berlin. The city was given a huge architectural scheme with massive structures as a result from the Nazi regime. The goal was to completely change Berlin as the capital city with the highest quality on earth.

The Olympic Games of 1936 hosted by Nazi Germany were the greatest opportunity to display to the world the progress made by the nation. All kinds of athletes from around the world traveled to Berlin and participated in a variety of sporting events. Many of them performed the Nazi salute during the beginning ceremony. Hitler projected in the eyes of foreigners the image of an enlightened Germany that had escaped the terrible past and looked forward to an optimistic future. This was, in turn, a direct signal to the world's enemies, as well as an effort to put the fear in their hearts when they saw the Nazi potential. However, this message was not well-received by Great Britain and France, who were unaware of the real motives behind Hitler's foreign policy.

Hitler intended to teach the young Germans in Hitler's Nazi ideology. He therefore paid particular focus on the younger generationbecause he believed that through their influence the regime would last for a longer time, possibly for a thousand years. Thus, he established Hitler's Youth, an organization that was created with the intention of imposition of the Nazi method of thinking on youngsters. When they reached at the age of 6 young boys were sent to camps where they were trained according to the Nazi method. They had to undergo strict physical training, since they were first prepared for the SA as well as later to join eventually for Wehrmacht (the German Army). In 1939, 90% of German teenagers were Hitler's teens.

Girls were not left out from their Nazi regime, since the party had planned something special for girls. Hitler established his own League of German Girls, which was in fact the female arm of his Youth. The League was divided into various groups, such as that of the Young Girls League (for girls aged between ten and fourteen years old) older) and a different league that was for girls who were between fourteen and 18 years old. In

1938, a third part was introduced to the club named The Faith and Beauty League, which was available to girls aged between 17 and 21 years old. The purpose of this section was helping these girls prepare for careers as well as domestic life and wedding, since they were encouraged to marry young and have children but they had to get an education first, and then a job as soon as it was possible. This was because Hitler was determined to establish the foundations and plant in the seed of Nazi movement and its ideology to the future generations.

Chapter 6: Building The Power Of Military

"There is no unity in Europe It is all submission" -- Adolf Hitler to Otto Strasser in 1927.

A) Infringing on the Treaty of Versailles

According to Hitler The Treaty of Versailles was one of the most humiliating events in German history because it the treaty did not just mean the surrender to Germany (which did not defeat at the battle) However, it also brought extremely severe sanctions against Germany. There were significant territorial loss for Germany like that of Alsace in the region of Alsace and Lorraine to France which was a huge area in East Prussia and Upper Silesia were lost to the favor of Poland The city of Danzig was declared a liberated city. Saarland was put under the control by the League of Nations and all the German colonies in across the Pacific, China, and Africa were given in the hands of Great Britain, France, and Japan.

When the Allies were taking on Germany accountable for conflict, the Allies also ordered enormous reparation cost to compensate the harm that the German Army caused in World War I. In 1921 the total costs of reparations were estimated at 33 billion dollars a figure that was unprecedented at the period. The treaty also granted the Allies the ability to intervene should the Germans were to retaliate with their payments like it was the situation that the French and Belgians did in the Ruhr region of Ruhr between January 11, 1923 until August 25, 1925. The French were determined to stop any possibility of German reprisals and to ensure that Germany was never a threat to military operations in Europe by restricting their German Army to a mere one hundred thousand troops and getting rid of the generals. Production of tanks, automobiles, planes, submarines as well as poisonous gas was totally banned, with only few factories allowed to make ammunition and weapons. Additionally, the entire Rhineland was to be disarmed. This treaty also led to the establishment of the League of Nations, which was an organization that was very similar to the present UN with the idea that members were required to guarantee the territorial integrity and independence of all other members. The primary goal that was the sole purpose of the League of Nations was to keep peace.

Anyone who is a German nationalist is deeply shocked by the harsh sanctions imposed upon Germany through the Allies and the treaty led to massive social uprisings. This treaty was in actual the birth certificate of extreme nationalist movement within Germany and was the cause of the rise and the rise of The Nazi party. When the German populace was being afflicted by unemployment and the severe austerity measures enforced through the Weimar Republic, they were seeking an official figure to break the Treaty of Versailles and to make amends for the harm that was inflicted on Germany. Hitler and the other German nationalists refused to accept the surrender of Germany, particularly since its army was never defeated in battle and they believed that they were being cheated by the German Army was being swindled by cowardly politicians, who Hitler would call"the "criminals who were a part of the November Revolution". Although Germany's surrender was difficult to take and they were unable to accept it, the Treaty of Versailles was, actually, the catalyst that triggered social uprisings. Since his election campaign in 1929, Hitler promised to break the Treaty of Versailles and lead Germany back to its glory days.

In the Nazi doctrine it was believed that the pure German was regarded as a superior race to other nations, including those of East. East (which Hitler hated so that he did not only hate Jews and the other Slavic nationalities, against which he had been expressing a growing dislike since the time which he lived at Vienna). The goal of Fuhrer was to expand the Lebensraum that was the area of living for the German population by conquering new territories, and eliminating or make slaves of the population that was already inferior. The only way to achieve this goal was to be accomplished through war which, in addition to breaking the Treaty of Versailles but also infringed on the rules of the League of Nations (of which Germany was an active member).

Since the Nazis were elected to the power of Germany, they offered jobs to unemployment-ridden Germans They were able to keep their word with the unemployment rate dropping by six percent to one million. The Nazis rehabilitated the infrastructure, however most of the jobs were at factories, which were required to produce ammunition, weapons, tanks aircrafts, submarines and ships, as well as other war-related machinery. Hitler restored the manufacturing of weapons using Mefo bill (a promissory note that was issued by the German Central Bank). Additionally, during this time it was during this time that the Nazi administration printed lots of money. They also confiscated the wealth of many Jews as well as wealthy enemies of the state.

The year 1933 was the time that Germany was able to withdraw from the League of Nations and didn't attend the World Disarmament Conference in October 1933. This should have sent a clear signal for the rest of the world to know that Germany was in the process of preparing for war. However, the big powers did not react, and they did not react when 90% of the population of Saarland (which fell under the supervision under the League of Nations) voted for Unification with Germany in January 1935. The most direct breach against the Treaty of Versailles was the rise in the Wehrmacht in March 1935 in which Hitler was not afraid to declare the

German Army included more than 6 million soldiers which was six times greater than the limit established under the Treaty. With the aid of industry, Nazis created an organization called the Luftwaffe (German Air Forces) as well as The Kriegsmarine (The Germany Navy). Another infraction was the reoccupation and retaking of the Rhineland that was the present time a demilitarized zone. In the meantime, the Great Powers were watching passively as the Germans were breaking article after article of the Treaty of Versailles. In August 1936 Hitler ordained Hermann Goring to implement the Four Year Plan, which was intended in order to improve the preparation of Germany for war over the coming four years.

B) New Alliances

In contrast to domestic politics, where Hitler was not a fan of any allies, he was conscious that he needed to create alliances in the event of war to come, when it came with foreign affairs. The first nation Hitler considered he should take on was Italy and he found the source of his source of inspiration from Benito Mussolini, the undisputed supreme ruler of Italy. The attempt to take power in 1923 was influenced from the "March on Rome," an action which resulted in the naming of Benito Mussolini the PrimeMinister of Italy. In the year 1923, Hitler and his Nazi supporters were attempting to take over the power of Bavaria and then marched on Berlin to take on the ruling party at the time. In the event, this plan failed. Hitler who was in prison for high treason was able to show a lot of respect and sympathy to Il Duce (Benito Mussolini's nickname). He had been seeking to join forces with Il Duce from the 1920s onward, but only when he was named chancellor and auto-proclaimed himself Fuhrer could he begin to make plans to form alliances. As the Fuhrer was in the process of preparing to fight, his very first person to consider was Mussolini since he believed Il Duce was his natural Ally.

The two leaders of the political world first met on the 25th of October in 1936. The two leaders formed a strong bond and concluded a treaty of partnership which was titled "The Axis," after the words of Benito Mussolini which stated that all European nations would rotate around an "Rome-Berlin Axis." Just one month after, Germany signed an anti-communist accord with Japan that was referred to informally as the Anti-Comintern Pact. Italy was to join the agreement only later in the year 1937. The Axis was transformed into an alliance for military purposes in 1939, and after Japan becoming a member in the year 1940 it was renamed known as the Tripartite Pact. Hitler and Mussolini made an appearance during the Spanish Civil War, both leaders assisting General Franco. Although Mussolini was looking to end the war in the event of General Franco winning, Hitler just wanted to keep the conflict in the process. Italy provided more than 750,000 troops, whereas Germany contributed a smaller contribution.

The French were determined to reduce the power of an emerging Germany in recognition of the power that it had. They knew that Germany was in the process of rearmament and also observed the Germans in the Rhineland. However the French were not keen to engage directly in war, and instead, they formed the alliance of Soviet Russia in order to reduce the Nazi threat to Central Europe. Following this partnership, Hitler hated the French further, because he believed they were threatening the entire continent of Europe in signing the treaty to the Soviets.

Unexpectedly, a different country Hitler was hoping to make an all-weather ally would be Great Britain. After his imprisonment and imprisoned, it was believed that the Fuhrer was adamant about forming an alliance Great Britain, as it is portrayed in his memoir, Mein Kampf. Even though it was a country that criticized the Fuhrer's violation and infringements of the Treaty of Versailles, Great Britain didn't take any actions against Germany. Hitler believed that having an agreement with British could be possible and he wasn't. On the 18th of June 1935 the Anglo-German Naval Agreement was signed in a document that permitted for the German Navy to increase in size, yet limit it to just 35 % of the British Navy. It was regarded as a major accomplishment by the Fuhrer who believed that this was the first step toward an American-German Alliance. But, in 1937 Hitler had to quit his plans for an alliance, placing the blame to his British leadership.

c) A Bigger Germany

The expansion of The Lebensraum was among Hitler's top goals because there was plenty of areas to conquer, where the German citizens could live and the native people were being wiped out or forced into slavery. It was the first task to restore the borders of Germany in the same way they were at the close in World War I before signing the Treaty of Versailles. In the meantime, Saarland was already part of the German territory as well as it was the Rhineland is under German control for the first time. The simplest method to allow Germany to expand was to unify with Austria. On the 12th of March 1938 Hitler announced the unification of Austria together with Germany as Anschluss. The process was without any bloodshed and Hitler was able to return home as the triumphant liberator. The Nazi army was welcomed and applauded by the Austrian citizens.

The next item on the list of targets for Hitler was Czechoslovakia in which German ethnic minorities dominated that region. Sudetenland region. The Fuhrer wasn't just interested in the region, He wanted to conquer the entire nation to be conquered. The Fuhrer attended a few discussions with leading politicians from the Sudeten German Party (which was the biggest German ethnics-based party in the region) in which they discussed a plan to take on Czechoslovakia. The party demanded more freedom from

Czechoslovakian government, but its main goal was to create violent clashes with the police. Since the government complied with every one of the Sudeten German Party demands and a number of violent confrontations took place between German ethnics under the instructions by the Sudeten German Party as well as police from the Czechoslovakian Police. The result was the instillation for martial law within a few districts of Sudeten district, and provided Hitler the reason to enter to defend the German ethnic minorities from Czechoslovakian authorities. Because Germany relied upon British energy, Hitler couldn't act immediately but he directed the Wehrmacht to begin preparing Fall Grun (Case Green) in April 1938. Since it was evident that the Great Powers were aware of the tensions within the Sudeten region there was a peace conference called, which resulted in the admission of Sudetenland to Germany. The conference took place in Munich on the 29th of September 1938. The gathering was attended by the premier of Great Britain (Neville Chamberlain) as well as the premier secretary of France (Edouard Daladier) as well as Benito Mussolini. The British prime minister was satisfied with the results of the peace conference but he didn't know about Hitler's plans. The Fuhrer faced his foes and this made him more determined to go after his military goals and foreign adversaries, since they were convinced of their inaction and insanity to take action. It was a difficult time for the German economy was in an extremely challenging time, because the preparations for war consumed lots of material resources as well as raw substances. Germany required to increase its exports to fund the basic materials needed to run its business (it was in huge demand for iron to construct all the components in the German war machine (including aircrafts, battleships and tanks guns, weapons along with ammunition).

But, he also believed that a country in the vicinity of Czechoslovakia might possess additional sources of iron and other raw materials, and so he directed the Wehrmacht to begin the invasion of the country and to break the Munich agreement. In March, German troops invaded the country and on March 16 Hitler declared from the Prague Castle that Bohemia and Moravia were now under German Protectorate. Hitler made these two provinces as part of the German Lebensraum in the sense that Bohemia and Moravia were part of the German Lebensraum for many thousands of years. In this moment, it was evident that to Great Britain and France that Hitler was not someone who could be negotiated with, because his motives were explicit, and he was going to not rest until he had achieved his objectives. The governments that were passive in these nations didn't take steps to end Hitler at the start since they didn't feel prepared to face a direct battle. If they wanted to avoid Germany and the Wehrmacht, they would find out that the Wehrmacht came to them.

Chapter 7: The Leader Of A War Machine

"I will make them a devil's beverage" -- Adolf Hitler reacting to the British "guarantee" regarding Polish independence.

A) the Greater Germanic Reich

The 1st of September, 1939 began the first day the beginning of World War II, a conflict that would take many lives of people, not just soldiers as well as civilians. And that's not even including the Holocaust which resulted in the annihilation of 6 millions of European Jews, approximative two-thirds of the Jewish population of Europe. To expand Lebensraum, Hitler was determined to extend Lebensraum, Hitler was also determined to win back the land belonging to East Prussia, now being under Polish administration. In the summer of 1939 Hitler felt he was required to take action in order to achieve his goal, believing of the fact that Great Britain was his biggest enemy, and that the invading of Poland was only one step toward achieving the ultimate objective. August 1939 was a time of pacts and alliances like the Molotov Ribbentrop Pact (a non-aggression agreement between Germany and the Soviet Union signed between the foreign ministers of both nations on August 23, 1939) as well as the Anglo-Polish Alliance of August 25 1939. Hitler had reason to believe that Mussolini was not going to honor the alliance he had signed with Nazi Germany however, he delayed the attack for a couple of days as he planned to take over Poland on the 25th of August. This invasion into Poland began on September 1 1939. It was the perfect chance for Germany to show its superiority on all levels.

Poland was not a match for Germany because the Luftwaffe was unstoppable from the skies. The Wehrmacht could move quickly, and the German battleships were able attack Polish ports that were within the reach the guns. The plan was simple: the Wehrmacht could clear the way for the SS soldiers would follow (an organization that was founded with originally been created to defend Hitler however, their work was later shifted to intelligence, and eventually operating prison camps). Their objective to do this in Poland was to make the Polish population German by searching for non-Germans and Jewish individuals. Jews were often killed , or eventually branded. In Poland the SS have committed the most horrific crimes against the Jewish community, due to having in the ghettos of Poland, massive Jewish Ghettos as well as the horrible concentration camps. Hitler's main motive to conquer Poland was to win back the territory in East Prussia and to claim the city that was free of Danzig (Gdansk as it is referred to in Polish). Poland was a prize that was easy to secure to Nazi Germany. But, it wasn't without consequences. Great Britain and France finally declared war on Germany on September 3rd, 1939. However, they did not launch an offensive against German troops or Germany. Hitler could easily have a plan for how to conduct the purge of the social order in Poland which would ultimately result in the death many millions Jews. On April 9 of 1940 Hitler attacked Denmark and Norway and a months later, Hitler began his assault upon France, Belgium, Luxembourg along with the Netherlands. Mussolini only joined the war at the end of June, 1940 and on June 22nd on the 22nd of June 1944, France was able to surrender and signed the armistice. Hitler had just enacted one of his goals which was the establishment of the Greater Germanic Reich, which brought together the nations of racial purity comprising Scandinavian, Dutch and Flemish under German control. Similar to Poland, Hitler ran a Germanization strategy, which is why the SS were able to target people who are Jews from Denmark, Norway, Belgium, Luxembourg and the Netherlands. To satisfy himself, Hitler restored the same train coach that was used to sign the armistice, signed on 11 November 1918 was signed. Hitler urged French officials to sign at this moment the formal surrender to France. It was the time when British troops were ordered by the French to go back England after the beach of Dunkirk.

Hitler was extremely pleased with the results of the war to date He even made twelve generals of his army to field marshals. Because of their efforts that France was defeated earlier than Hitler was expecting, hence the concept of Blitzkrieg was employed to describe the war in France. The Luftwaffe was able to offer air support to the Wehrmacht and was completely unaffected by the skies. But, things were going to change for German Air Forces, because Hitler was planning to strike Great Britain by air. In the

Battle of Britain was the battle with both the British Royal Air Force and the German Luftwaffe and the German Luftwaffe suffered heavy losses. While it was equipped with more aircrafts as compared to those of the Royal Air Force, the Luftwaffe was outsmarted by experienced and determined British pilots. They were able to defeat the British air force's fighter plane Supermarine Spitfire was more powerful than its counterpart, the German Messerschmitt BF 109, which resulted in devastating losses to the Luftwaffe. It was the Battle of Britain was lost, Hitler suffering his first defeat of World War II. Because the German Navy was unable to compete with the British Navy, a complete land assault on Britain was not in the cards. Hitler decided to go for night air attacks, bombing the biggest cities in Great Britain. The strategy lasted for months, and among cities that the Luftwaffe struck included London, Coventry, and Plymouth.

It was reported that the German forces were stopped in the British Channel, as the Nazis were unable to further move towards the West. Hitler was now forced to focus on the Eastern portion of Europe in order to conquer more territory in order to benefit his German people, and in addition, to overthrow the Bolshevik government that was led by Joseph Stalin. Since Hitler was able to win Japan to be an all-alliance, the other Eastern European countries joined him. So, Hungary, Romania, and Bulgaria joined the forces of Hitler in the fight against Russia and the Soviet Union. In the end of November, 1940 Hitler began to plan to strike his Soviet Union. The year 1941 was the time when Hitler was still invading countries , such as Yugoslavia and then Greece as well as Crete. Nazi troops also aided troops of the Italians on the continent of Lybia (Northern African region) and the Iraqi rebels fighting British forces. So, German troops were present in Northern Africa, the Balkans as well as in the Middle East as the conflict was spreading more rapidly than the war before.

Churchill was the one who made Hitler to stop on his position on the English Channel and also managed to end his Western Front in Europe. This could be seen as an important turning point in the War as it brought the first major German loss on the field and showed the people that Luftwaffe wasn't invincible. In the end, RAF stood as the sole thing standing in the way of Hitler and his triumph in

Western Europe. If the Germans were to have prevailed it would have likely meant the conclusion of the war but the war lasted for almost five years. The Fuhrer had to give up his claims against the British and concentrate on his areas within Eastern Europe, lands which were crucial to the Lebensraum. Another front was also opened within Northern Africa, where the Nazis as well as their Italians engaged in a war with Allied forces to take control of the region. At the time, German troops were already fighting on three continents, an extremely difficult war effort to sustain in terms of manpower and resources.

B) A Final Solution

The source of anti-Semitism was not in the aftermath from World War I, as the hatred of Jews began some centuries. In large areas of Europe it was believed that the Jewish group was among the richest, since they were merchants with a high-end reputation who were more wealthy and influential (in some cases) than the majority of the population. In the past, it was thought that Jews had control over the banks of Europe and also expanded their influence on the political class and other large segments that dominated the market. While some might think the notion that Hitler was anti-Semitic since his teens however it was the time which he was in Vienna which sparked his hatred of this nation. In the Austro-Hungarian Empire of the past, he observed the struggles for the German ethnic group, since they were forced to reside in the same state, with 11 different nationalities. Additionally the ideology that the empire had was one of favoring Slavic nations, which meant that the German population was disadvantaged due to this policy. But the biggest danger for them came from their Jewish population (according to the majority of German nationalists) because it was so influential and powerful that it was preventing the growth for the German population (most of them were working classes, while Jews were middle and upper class).

It was the hatred for Jews as well as all other ethnic groups in Vienna that grew Hitler's resentment towards the Austro-Hungarian Empire as well as its capital city. When he was exposed to anti-Semitic discourse He believed strongly that Jews were infiltrating the upper levels of financial and political positions. In the aftermath of Germany's surrender, Germany following World War I was also an additional cause to be blamed on the Jews since Hitler believed that they were among the traitors accountable for the armistice of November 1918 as well as the Treaty of Versailles. As a passionate German Nationalist Hitler pledged to correct the mistakes that had been done by that ceasefire armistice as well as the Treaty of Versailles, and equally to punish harshly those he believed were responsible for the humiliation that was imposed on Germany. The time following the war included bloody political protests as a variety of radical groups tried to take over the power of Germany. One of them was that of the German Workers Party (DAP) that had a radical approach to Marxists as well as Jews. Hitler believed that this was the place the best fit was, therefore he joined the party and, within a brief time, he was the party's undisputed leader. At the time it was a very tense political climate and to ensure security at public gatherings of the party or simply to intimidate political opposition, Hitler had to create an organization of paramilitary soldiers to serve like"the "iron finger" for the group. In the meantime The German Workers' party was now"the National Socialist German Worker's Party or, in other words it was the Nazi party. The paramilitary group was known as the SA and was a part of its role in the Nazi party for a long time however, in the course of time Hitler was unable to trust the organization because it became very unruly and difficult to manage and not discrete. This is why Hitler came up with the SS that was initially designed to serve as his personal guard however in the coming years it would take on an increasingly important function.

The future of this group was to be defined in the hands of Heinrich Himmler, who joined in 1925, and then took over the management over the SS in 1929. He overhauled the organization, and made into one of Germany's most formidable and fearsome paramilitary forces in Germany. The purpose that the SS was not that important initially, serving as bodyguards to Hitler as well as other Nazi high-ranking leaders, but by using them Hitler recognized a efficient group that could carry out his visions for Nazi Germany. Thus the SS was entrusted with important tasks such as surveillance, intelligence and security and surveillance and spreading terror across Germany as well as the territories that were occupied. The number of members grew rapidly to the point that by 1933, the organization was home to greater than 290000 employees. The recruits they recruited were meticulously chosen, as they needed to demonstrate their Aryan background , and also obtain documents that proved their ancestry going all from the 1800s or 1750s. A large part of the Nazi policies regarding race was set forth through the Nuremberg Laws which were passed by the Reichstag on September 15th in 1935. As per these laws only those of German blood were considered to be citizens in the Reich and anyone who had 3 or more Jewish grandparents were considered to be a Jew. The union between the blood of a Jew or a person with German blood was prohibited as was sexual relations between Jews. The same laws were also applicable on the Romani community as well as people of German descent. Black Germans.

The SS comprised two distinct entities: The Allgemeine SS and the Waffen SS. The first was in charge of implementing Hitler's racist policies, while the second of them was an elite combat squad that was part of to the Wehrmacht during the conflict. A third element of the SS was later founded and was called the SS-Totenkopfverbande, which was the group responsible for running the concentration camps.

Heinrich Himmler soon became one of Hitler's most trusted henchmen his actions and those of SS could have a devastating impact on the populace of Europe. He was appointed the chief of police in the outside of Prussia and was also the deputy of Himmler, Reinhard Heydrich was appointed the head of the Gestapo and also held the title as the chief of the Security Service (SD). In order to "start the fire" against the Jewish community, Hitler needed a spark. On the 7th of November of 1938, the German diplomat Ernst von Rath was killed by an Polish Jew named Herschel Grynszpan at the German Embassy in Paris. A few days later, vom Rath died and provided to the Nazi authorities the best chance to begin a large-scale attack against Jews. Between November 9 and 10 on the 9 and 10 of November, the SS, SA, and as well as German civilians launched attacks on Jews. In excess of seven hundred thousand Jewish storefronts were destroyed, and more than a thousand synagogues were destroyed and burned to the floor. Ninety Jews were murdered, and thirty thousand were deported to concentration camps at Dachau, Sachsenhausen, and Buchenwald. The majority of Jews that were taken to these camps were later released, but 21,000 were kept in camps. The entire operation was known as Kristallnacht and, although it did not cause a lot of deaths, it was the end of Jewish cultural and public life. For certain Jews it was the obvious indication that it was the time to go to Germany.

In 1939, the entire security and police forces were integrated into one unit that was referred to as"the Reich Main Security Office, which was led by Reinhard Heydrich. Hitler believed in Himmler the ideal person to enforce his racist policies because he held the same opinions towards Jews as well as other ethnic groups. Himmler along with his deputy (Heydrich) launched the genocide of at 6 millions of Jews as well as more than 10 million additional deaths of various ethnic groups such as Soviets, Romani, Serbs gay men, and many others.

In the war of invasion where the Wehrmacht was to go and the SS would follow, launching the policy of ethnic cleansing. At first they killed those who were "socially impure" parts of the population. However, when they encountered huge amounts of Jews who were Jewish, they decided that they should label them them and make them live in ghettos following the removal of their belongings. Since the number of detained Jews was rising rapidly and increasing, the SS needed to find the most effective strategy to eliminate the Jews. That's the reason that concentration camps first appeared within Operation Reinhard (named after Himmler's deputy who was the chief architect of this plan). There were several major concentration camps, the majority of them in Poland. They included Auschwitz, Belzec, Chelmno, Majdanek, Maly Trostinets, Sobibor, and Treblinka. In these camps they were where the Nazis would unleash terror upon the Jews and the Jews were made to work in an inhumane conditions until they exhausted and later taken to large rooms in which they were executed with toxic gas such as Zyklon-B Hydrogen cyanide and prussic gas.

The majority of Jews that were murdered in these camps were of Poland (around 2.1 millions), Soviet Union (approximately the same amount) and Hungary (more than half one million Jews). The concentration camps that killed the most people included Auschwitz, Treblinka, and Belzec with more than 1.1 million of, between 870 and 600 000 Jews who were killed. In the territories that were occupied there were a few Jews as well as other groups of ethnicity weren't able to get to the concentration camps as they were killed in the site. Tens of thousands were murdered through this method, but in other circumstances there were other situations where the Nazis were given orders to starve the inhabitants of the area and to provide food and other supplies to the Germans. Reinhard Heydrich was killed in 1942 by an armed small group made up of Czech partisans, however this didn't affect the goals of annihilating Jews as well as other groups of ethnicity. In the summer of 1943, it was evident that the Germans were going to be defeated in the war. But this didn't stop the murders. Josef Mengele, an SS officer, and also a doctor at Auschwitz executed dangerous experimentation on human beings Jews. This is the reason he earned the moniker "Angel of Death."

In all in all, the SS were responsible for murder of more than six million Jews and seven millions Soviets (of the latter, 1.3 million of them were Soviets Jews) and two or three millions Soviet prisoners, 1.8-1.9 million Poles, between 300 and 500 thousand Serbs about 200 000 to 220 000 Romani. They did not show mercy to gay, disabled males, or Jehovah's Witnesses by killing numerous of them.

Every other human tragedy in history is not as dramatic as the genocide committed by the Jewish people, as well as different ethnic communities. The massive depopulation of regions in Central as well as Eastern Europe, to create an area to accommodate to accommodate the German populace to colonize. About two-thirds of the Jewish population of Europe was destroyed, while the rest managed to escape the persecution from the Nazi regime. After the war, a lot of Jews moved to the present-day state of Israel as a new state that began to grow in the years following the war, creating huge tensions and conflict with a few Arab states. Middle East was as hostile to Jews like Nazi Germany was during World War II However, Holocaust is regarded as Holocaust was considered by every Jew to be the greatest tragedy in their entire history.

Though most people is aware of the Holocaust the fact is that anti-Semitism wasn't gone after the end of World War II and anti-Semitic views are still prevalent particularly during times of economic turmoil.

C) Turning Point Turning Point

Hitler never ceased to have the aim to destroy his Soviet Union and wiping out the communist ideology. the man he was hated by Marxists just as he disliked Jews. In addition he believed the development of Communism was funded with the help of wealthy Jewish bankers in an attempt to destroy Russian Empire and, more importantly, represented a risk to the entirety of Europe. However, he didn't target his country's Soviet Union repeatedly as he was focused on the destruction of those who were the Western Great Powers. When he realized that Great Britain couldn't be invaded and he turned his focus toward the East in which there were plenty of land to allow German individuals to establish. There were in addition, certain Slavic nations that he resented the most, and perhaps more importantly, a lot of Jews. Since he saw them as to be a subhuman race, Hitler was determined to eradicate these countries out of Europe. It was accomplished through the destruction of Yugoslavia and Ukraine two Slavic countries, in which Hitler would have wanted to eradicate huge portions of the indigenous people, not just Jews. At this moment the Fuhrer had a lot of allies like Hungary, Romania, and Bulgaria and Romanian oil did not provide fuel for the German war machine. In the end, Hungarian, Romanian and Bulgarian Army joined forces with the Germans because it was evident the fact that Hitler had plans to attack into the Soviet Union.

On June 22nd, 1941 Hitler started the war on the Soviet Union, conquering countries such as that of Baltic Republics, Belarus and West Ukraine. The attack was planned to be carried out on three fronts, including a west one in Leningrad (modern-day Sankt Petersburg) as well as a central one that would be directed towards Moscow and the southern one via Kiev. The idea was to strike Moscow from three different angles and result in that the surrender of Soviets. But, at this stage, Hitler was somehow convinced that he was a brilliant tactician , and often was not in agreement with his generals about the strategy to follow. After having pushed about 5100 kilometers over enemy territory, both the Germans along with the Russians finally fought in the Battle of Smolensk (Soviet resistance did not end this German advances). The battle was the biggest victory for German troops. Germans in the Eastern front, however it was preceded by poor decisions from Hitler. The Fuhrer had directed that the Centre Army Group to stop its advance and help to the German soldiers on opposite areas, Western and Southern, because Hitler was determined to take on Leningrad in Leningrad and Kiev. Leningrad and Kiev were the main targets. Centre Army Group was just 400 miles from Moscow and the command to stop the march wasn't an order that generals backed, therefore there was a rift within the ranks of the German military leaders. This provided the perfect occasion for the Soviet troops to be mobilized and to prepare to defend Moscow. In the Eastern front, this was one of the major errors. The advance only got reaffirmed in the month of October 1941, but the massive invasion and assault against Moscow on three sides never going to take place. The weather conditions were significantly much worse when German tanks were sunk in the mud and as they moved further into enemy territory the tanks were beginning running out of food. Winter was the most difficult time for Hitler due to the fact that the German tanks or soldiers weren't equipped to handle the harsh weather conditions. The full-scale assault on Moscow could have brought about the final victory of the war, with an Nazi victory. For the Allies the war was essential to Hitler to lose at Moscow.

The assault on Moscow was dubbed Operation Typhoon ended very badly for the Germans because the attack was a failure in and of itself. Stalin mobilize soldiers from Siberian as well as Far Eastern territories to defend Moscow, and also erected three zones of defense outside Moscow and managed to deter the Germans from moving further. They also put together an offensive that was successful in pushing Hitler's troops away from the villages in Oryol, Vyazma, and Vitebsk. The Soviet forces were extremely close to encircling those three German armies. The Fuhrer took the matter to his own and named himself the chief leader for German troops. This was a huge defeat for Germany's Wehrmacht since it could not achieve any major victory for the rest of its life. The year 1942 was the beginning in World War II when Nazi troops were losing battle after battle.

In their efforts to take control of Egypt as well as the Suez canal In their efforts to control the Suez canal and Egypt, Germans were defeated in their attempts to control the Suez canal. Germans fell to British during the battles of El Alamein (twice) and Alam el Halfa, preventing the Italian-German forces from moving into Egypt and gaining control of the Suez Canal. The battle culminated in the Battle of Stalingrad from August 1942 until February 1943. The offensive in Stalingrad was proceeding according to plan, with the Luftwaffe was able to successfully bomb the city, and The Wehrmacht was able push out the Soviet troops. However it was the Soviet forces began Operation Uranus, with the strategy of flanking Axis forces, focusing on smaller Romanian as well as Hungarian armies. The strategy worked in that the Soviet forces were able to take over their German troops in an effort to end their source of supply. The battle nearly killed all of the German 6th Army, as the Axis troops suffered massive losses during the most bloody battle during the entire war. More than half a million soldiers died and over 600 000 soldiers were wounded or seriously ill. Hitler refused to yield the city's control which is why he instructed to the 6th Army to stand its stand and maintain Stalingrad in German control. In February 1943, the Axis forces were running low on supplies and were forced give up their positions in surrender to the Soviet Army. Over 265 000 soldiers surrendered , and the Russian forces captured them as prisoners. The loss was a crushing hit to those fighting for the Axis forces, who lost countless lives, as well as many airplanes, tanks and weapons. The Wehrmacht already lost a lot of soldiers, however the German propaganda succeeded in convincing citizens of Germany to join the war. The troops were not disciplined and the training required for war, which meant they weren't very useful to the Fuhrer.

The Battle of Stalingrad was considered as the turning point during World War II, as it dealt the German forces a crushing blow. German forces. The Wehrmacht were in an area of retreat and did not even think of advancing towards Moscow. This was the start of the end for German troops as it signaled Allied forces to fight the Nazis and to open new fronts like those in Italy and then to open the Western front in the Normandy campaign (or Operation Overlord). The Axis troops were required to alter their tactics, shifting from a large-scale offensive to a more aggressive defensive.

Chapter 8: After The War

The newly established German republic was that was in chaos. Right-wing nationalists , also known as Freikorps (ex-soldiers to be hired) were at war with left-wing Marxists and other groups, each with their own views on the future of a nation which was then becoming a republic. The Germans were apathetic, if not completely ignorant information about republics, as they had been under the monarchy for hundreds of years.

There was no one left protected during this time of turmoil from socialists to communists and in January 1919, a lot of innocent civilians were killed in Berlin as well as others later in the month of May in Munich.

The German General Staff (army) offered its assistance in eradicating Marxism and also ensuring order. In return, the fledgling democracy, which was just beginning to emerge, let the military generals keep their honor and status.

On June 28th 1919, 1919 On June 28, 1919, the Allies agreed to sign The Treaty of Versailles. This was intended to punish those nations that were defeated in the war.

Treaty of Versailles[2Treaty of Versailles[2

Germany was the sole party responsible for the war.

Germany was required to compensate for the damages, which was PS6,600 million, which was set a few months after the signature of the agreement.

The army was reduced to 100,000 troops. The tanks were not allowed.

The navy was limited to six ships, but no submarines.

Germany was not permitted to have to have an air force.

The Rhineland region was intended to be free of German soldiers and weapons.

Germany was not permitted to be a part of Austria. Her land was also confiscated by several other nations:

France has taken over Alsace-Lorraine.

Belgium was the first to take Eupen as well as Malmedy.

Denmark was granted North Schlweswig.

Czechoslovakia as well as Poland also received land.

The League of Nations took control of the German colonies, most particularly within East Africa, the territory that is now Tanzania.

According to the conditions of the treaty Germany alone was responsible for the war and was required to cover all costs. The Germans were not thrilled by the war, as they saw the war as another humiliation to their country, and Hitler later appealed to the people by saying that he would tear it down.

German Workers"Party

"Our battle is with money. Working alone can aid us but not money. We must end the slavery of interest. We must fight the races that symbolize money."

Following after the end of the war Germany changed into a democracy. However, the radical change from monarchy to democratic system did not please the masses as political parties popped out and each one with a plan to win power using any meansnecessary, and to restore the glory and glory lost by their nation. It was the German General Staff was in charge of to keep radical parties under control. Hitler was employed as an informant in Munich in the year 1919. He was charged with conducting an investigation and reporting on a largely unnoticed section of"the German Worker's Party.

On September 12, 1919 Hitler was a guest at the German Workers Party for the very first time in a civilian dress. civilians. The event occurred in the basement of the Munich beer hall with around twenty to twenty five persons. There, he got the opportunity to hear the speech of Gottfried Feder . what means can capitalism be eradicated?

Then, Hitler was about to go when a person rose to speak. The person who spoke was in support of the dissolution from Bavaria of

Germany and the creation of a new nation along with Austria. Hitler adopts it from there and explains his response:

"At this point, I was compelled to take the floor and offering the gentleman my view regarding this issue. The result was that the last speaker had already done, left the room as a poodle that had gotten wet. When I had finished speaking to the crowd, they seen awed faces as they listened but only when I was about to thank the crowd and leave was a man soaring following me, introduce himself (I did not know the name) and then slap the small booklet in my hand it was a pamphlet for political purposes and a request for to go through it.'

The man who put the book into Hitler's hands is Anton Drexler, one of the founding members of the party. the publication was titled "My Political Awakening". Drexler saw the potential of the enthusiastic man who made his thoughts be known. Hitler had been invited back to join the same event.

In the morning, Hitler read the booklet and was delighted to find that it represented a lot of his ideasabout Drexler. Drexler (he himself was writer) had envisioned an anti-Semitic pro-military and nationalist party.

A terrible party invites Hitler to join

Hitler was able to make an impression on the people who were members the next few days when he received a message that he had been accepted as the new member. The party was at that point with little to talk about. The sentiments Hitler is a part of with his character in Mein Kampf:

'Wednesday came... ...Terrible, terrible! This was the life of a club in the most horrible manner and type. Should I join this club?

Following was the discussion of new memberships In another words, my capture was discussed.

I began to ask questions, but with the exception of a few guidelines I was able to find nothing, not a single program, leaflet or printed material in any way or membership cards, not even a terrible rubber stamp. It was just plain good will with good intention.'

This "stupid" organization that had none of a program, printed materials, or even membership cards would take the young, enthralled German nationalist to incredible heights in just four years. In the year 1923 Adolf Hitler had made himself famous and well-known in the sense that he believed that he could oust the government down with force through putsch. Putsch. But, first, the group required a major overhaul, including a name baptizing which is exactly the plan Hitler planned to do when he accepted the invitation to join after he was accepted at the age of thirty.

The German Workers' Part (Deutsche Arbeiterpartei, or DAP) was a small party at the time Hitler was elected in the month of September. He devised methods to influence and attract members by sending invitations to friends, to putting ads on an anti-Semitic Munich newspaper. Hitler also demanded that the meeting be moved from its current location to one with more capacity. The other participants were concerned, but they embraced his suggestion, relocating the public meeting into an underground beer cellar. More than

100 people attended at that time on the 16th of October 1919 gathering.

He is able to Sway by his Speech!

"Because it's to be inseparable from social thought and we are not convinced that there will ever be a permanent state of health if it's not based on social justice. Therefore, we've teamed up using this information."

Adolf Hitler

It was Hitler's first appearance as a speaker, as he was scheduled as the speaker with two speakers regardless of the fact that certain committee members were skeptical of his capabilities at the moment. It was an opportunity that a young Austrian boy had hoped to have in a small farm close to Linz. When the opportunity to speak and he sat down, he stepped up and was astonished to amaze everyone with his speech. He recounts the moment as Mein Kampf

I spoke for 30 minutes. What I simply felt inside me, but not ever knowing how was finally confirmed by the facts: I was able to speak! After 30 minutes, the people in the small space were captivated and their enthusiasm was first displayed by my plea to sacrifice for participants led to the donation of 300 marks.'

Hitler became the most popular speaker at German Workers' Party's meetings. He was the center of attention and the people who listened to him vent his unrestrained frustration and hatred over The Treaty of Versailles and blaming the Jews for the problems Germany faced including Germany's humiliating loss during World War I. The attendance slowly but surely rose to the point of a party to hundreds of people.

Hitler engaged soldiers he'd encountered while serving as a soldier, with aid from Ernst Rohm, an army captain. At Munich there were also ex-military members who were having a tough adjustment to the calm slow-going atmosphere - they also were part of the group. They all would make a huge impact on how well-known the event and its fame for being famous.

Party Make-over

In the beginning of 1920, Hitler took charge of the party's propaganda. In Februar of 1920, he advised that the German Workers' party organize its first general gathering.

The most prominent members of the party were strongly against the idea, believing that it was too early. Hitler thought it was a good idea to take the party- and perhaps himself upwards, to show the more powerful and popular Marxists that the German Workers' Party, he, Hitler and the German Workers were an organization to be reckoned with. He was aware that publicity would draw attention and, with that the party would gain membership.

He writes in Mein Kampf:

In the early 1920s I called for the organization of the first mass gathering. The meeting was not without controversy. Certain prominent party members considered the incident to be untimely and thus devastating in the end. The Red press began to be concerned about us, and we were lucky enough to gradually gain its disdain. We began to participate in discussions of other gatherings. Naturally, every one of us was immediately and screamed at. There washowever some progress. We were able to make friends with people and, as their knowledge of us increased, the anger and hatred towards us increased. So we were able to believe that at our first major mass gathering we would be greeted by many of our acquaintances of The Red group...

...And this is why that date, February 4 1920 was chosen for the date of the first mass gathering of the unidentified movement.

I personally supervised all the planning...

...On basis, the color red was selected because it's the most exciting color, and we were aware that it could cause a fury and anger to our adversaries most, and therefore draw their attention and recollections, regardless of whether they liked it or not.

On the 24th of February 1920, in the large room in Munich 2 000 people waited in line for Hitler to address the crowd.

He went on to explain the 25 principles from Hitler's Nazi party[3]

1. The unification among all Germans in the form of a Great Germany...

2. The German people enjoy rights similar to those of the other nations.

3. We are demanding land and territory (colonies)

4. The only people who... ...have German blood... ...can be our nation's citizens. Therefore, it is impossible for a Jew can qualify as a countryman.

5. The people who are not residents of the United States... ...must to be legally liable as foreigners.

6. The power to select the Government and decide on how laws are enforced by the state will be reserved to the citizens.

7. We ask that the state be the first to guarantee that all citizens have the

opportunity of living a decent life and earning a living...

8. Any future immigration of non-Germans is to be stopped.

9. Every citizen must have the same rights and duties.

10. The primary responsibility of every citizen is to be physically or mentally active.

So we ask:

11. The unearned earnings of all... ...be removed.

12. Because every war is a burden on the citizens... ...all individual profits resulting from war should be considered atrocity to the public. Therefore, we demand the complete confiscation of all war profit.

13. We want the nationalization of trusts in all countries.

14. We are requesting profit-sharing in the largest industries.

15. We want a substantial increase in pensions for old age.

16. We are calling for the development and preservation of a solid middle class...

17. We are requesting an agrarian reform that is in line with our national demands...

18. We demand that a ruthless combat be conducted against those who contribute against the public welfare.

19. We ask we demand that Roman law... ...be replaced by German common law.

20. We want to see children with poor parents... ...be taught with the help by the state.

21. The state has the obligation to improve the quality of health in the nation by providing maternity welfare facilities, interdicting child labor, and by improving physical fitness

22. We call for the dismantling of regular soldiers, and the establishment of an all-national (folk) military.

23. We demand legal action against those who promote deliberately falsehoods about politics and distribute these lies through the media. In order to facilitate the

establishment of an independent German newspaper, we ask:

(a) Editors and their assistants in publications published by the German language are German citizens.

(b) Newspapers from non-German countries can only be published with the explicit approval by the government. They are not permitted to publish in German language.

All financial interests in or impacting German newspapers will be prohibited to non-Germans in accordance with the legislation... ...Newspapers that are infringing against the general welfare will be shut down...

24. We want freedom for all religions within the State...

Common Good BEFORE Individual

25. In order to implement this plan, we require: the creation of a solid central authority within the State...The creation of professional committees as well as committees representing the various domains within the kingdom... These top

leaders of the party pledge to ensure the successful implementation of the above-mentioned issues at all cost and, if needed, with the risk of their lives.

Hitler explained each issue and received the approval of the crowd of groovy youngsters.

And when I finally handed the twenty-five theses point-for-point for point, to the masses and asked them to personally make a decision on them, one after the other was accepted with increasing excitement, all unanimously and unanimously... ...A flame was lit from its flame eventually the sword had to be drawn, restoring liberation for Germanic Siegfried, and the life of all the German nation.

Alongside the upcoming resurrection, I felt it was the god of unstoppable revenge for the shambles on November 9, 1919, was advancing.

The hall slowly was empty.

The movement developed its course.'

The movement had proved its own merits, with Hitler as its driving power behind it in the context of a Germany that was still facing uncertainty about its future. The sanctions enforced by the Allies caused economic hardship. The national pride was shattered. However, this young Austrian promised what a lot of people hoped for, something everyone desired: confidence.

The next action of Hitler was to provide the movement with a complete overhaul, as it didn't have a flag or symbol.

Nazi Party

(National sozialistische Deutsche Arbeiterpartei NSDAP).

"At the time of the genesis of the Movement we made the choice that we should give expression to this notion of the unity of two concepts regardless of any warnings and based on what we came to believe on the strength of our convictions and the conviction of our hearts, we named the movement "National Socialist. We told us that to be a "national is above all to show a unending and unconditional devotion to the people and, in the event of necessity even to sacrifice your life to protect it. Being a social is to improve the state and the society of the people . Every individual is acting in the interests of the entire community of people and should be in such a way confident of the goodness and of the integrity and honesty of this. group of people that they are willing to sacrifice everything for it."

- Adolf Hitler

As a young man from Lambach, Hitler had attended school at the Lambach Catholic Benedictine school. The stones had the carvings of swastikas and that's what Hitler chose as his symbol of his party. It was set in a white circle , with red backgrounds.

"In red we get the social vision of the movement, and in the white we see the idea of nationalism and in the swastika, the goal of fighting for the triumph of Aryan man and at same time, the triumph of the concept of creative work that is always anti-Semitic, and will remain anti-Semitic.'

Hitler changed the name of the party and the term 'National Socialist' was included, thus the full name was the National Socialist

German Workers' Party (Nationalsozialistische Deutsche Arbeiterpartei NSDAP). Nazi is short for "National Socialist.

Today, Adolf Hitler a highly effective in his capacity as a speaker. In the month of February in 1921, Hitler addressed before an audience of more than 6000 people inside Munich. People who were supporters of the Nazi Party had announced the gathering through a parade of shwastikas and handing out propaganda literature. This proved to be successful as Hitler gained recognition beyond those who were part of the Nazi Party.

The Munich Beer Hall Putsch

In the month of April 1921, Britain and France demanded the payment of Germany for the damage caused by the conflict. The result of these demands was the rise in the German mark. The German government sought an extension of the payment however France declined. Germany did not pay the bill. France took revenge in the beginning of January 1923, sending its military to the Ruhr Industrial Area of Germany.

The suffering citizens stood with their government in defiance to pay, until it began paying after September 1923. The result was a massive increase in inflation. As of November 1923 it was estimated that the German currency was worth 4,000,000,000 to the value of one U.S dollar. The people lost their savings, the money went into shambles and prices were absurdly high.

This angered the populace and the country erupted into chaos and extremist groups clamoring for the demise of the republic.

The Nazi party, which was based in Bavaria and Bavaria, enjoyed a huge fan base and Hitler was at present the head in the Nazi party.

Hitler considered this to be the opportunity he was waiting for and was confident that he was able to assume the presidency. The plan was to kidnap government officials at gunpoint and force them to swear their loyalty to Hitler as the future German leader.

"But when the shameful collapse happened and the devastating, shameful capitulation that followed, the loss of millions of marks as well as thousands of young Germans... ... Never was the moment more appropriate than it was in the moment when it cried out more loudly for an outcome than at the time when on one hand, the naked treason unabashedly exposed itself, while at the same time the people were economically driven to slow hunger.'

He solicited the help from World War I general Erich Ludendorff known as a respected and well-known person who would assist Hitler in gaining the support of his German Army. There was no way to fail and on the 8th of November 1923 Hermann Goring with an army of Nazi troops attacked the Munich beer hall where the heads from German government German government were in attendance..

It was a disaster when the State Commissioner Gustav von Kahr, head of the state police Lieutenant Colonel Hans von

Seisser, and commander of the German Army in Bavaria, General Otto von Lossow, pledged their loyalty to Hitler along with the Nazi party, then later, they retracted the pledge. This means that the police and the army didn't take part to participate in the Munich Beer Hall Putsch.

Hitler was detained and was tried for high Treason. It was supposed to be that he had ended his career as a politician. However, it turned out to be exactly the opposite as Hitler was the subject of a huge media coverage in his court trial. The judges were chosen from Nazi sympathizers. For a crime for which the sentence was life imprisonment, Hitler got only nine months. By the time he was about to get out, he'd written his autobiography Mein Kampf.

The New Man, Same Agenda

"The National Socialist Movement, in contrast will not allow its foreign policy to be dictated by the need to ensure the space that is essential for the existence of our people. It is not aware of Germanising or Teutonising like is the case with the national bourgeoisie, but rather the expansion of its

Folk. It won't observe in the subjugated, so-called Germanised, Czechs or Poles the national Folk, let alone a Folkish growing, but just the racial weakness of our Folk."

- Adolf Hitler

On December 19, 1924 Adolf Hitler was a liberated man after spending nine months of imprisonment. He came to freedom with a fresh outlook as the government was unable to be taken over through the force of arms, rather, the chance to be elected was legally.

Hitler made his way to freedom- in the form of a group that was facing many obstacles. The government had removed Hitler's Nazi Party. It also was struggling with internal conflicts. Never one to be overcome, Hitler decided to fix everything. And the first act he made at the beginning of the year 1925 was appeal to the premier of Bavaria to lift the ban. Then, he began reorganizing the party, particularly after the rally on February 27 where his ranting against the government led to him receiving a total exclusion from public speaking.

The Nazis divided Germany into 34 districts.

The Hitler Jugend, or Hitler Youth for teens aged between 15 and 18 was established.

The SA (Sturmabteilung) adopted their uniforms, which were brown shirts with a swastika-swathed armband, badges and a cap.

Within the SA the SA, a new security unit was created, dubbed the Schutzstaffel or SS. The highly disciplined unit, wearing a black uniform was the sole one responsible for the safety of Hitler in all times.

There was only one hurdle to overcome and that was the economic boom. People were no longer looking for someone who could promise them of a better future in exchange for their loyalty. It was a good time to support the German economy was growing.

The Lull; Hitler in Love

It was the Nazi party had gained prominence and power through appealing to hungry angry, frustrated and angry Germans. The situation was looking great, because of the United States which was giving the country loans, it seemed that there was no one to blame , and no reason to complain.

The nation was flourishing with borrowed money and time. All Hitler needed to do was sit and tie his time. While waiting, he ensured to improve his Nazi party to be prepared for any possibility. This was done through Joseph Goebbels, a highly educated and gifted person in the field of the art of organizing and making speeches. He was likely to have a significant impact on Nazi party's eventual rise to its peak. Hitler recognized that he required influence in Berlin as the centre of power in Germany. He sent Goebbels to Berlin in the month of October 1926.

In Berlin which was a city where the Nazi party was not as well-known as it was in Munich, Goebbels worked hard through the publication of newspapers, giving speeches at the meetings were organized by him, and placing posters throughout areas to scare off those Marxists that were dominant majority in Berlin. His efforts paid off as membership to the Nazi party grew.

The road was widened to accommodate Hitler. In 1927, he travelled to Berlin and, in front of a crowd of around 5,000 supporters delivered his speech. He captivated people with his emotional speech.

The elections occurred in Germany on the 20th of May, 1927. Goebbels efforts paid off and he was elected in the Reichstag however the Nazi party was not very successful at the polls.

The Nazi party was growing because of its appeal to discontented and desperate citizens , a time when the nation was suffering from the devastating results of losing- and also blaming of World War I. Now, things were improving; there was a flourishing and robust economy, industrialists had no debt, and the country had a president who was elected- Paul von Hindenburg who was the renowned World War I Field Marshal.

However Hitler's foresight, he warned of imminent dangerHowever, he faced personal issues of his own:

From his time of homelessness in Vienna to his barracks at the army, Hitler now had a location with a picturesque scene of Bavarian mountains. The year was 1928, and the 39-year-old invited his step-sister Angela to join at his new residence. Angela owned two children: Friedl as well as Geli. Adolf Hitler fell in love with his niece Geli who was half his age.

Hitler's overbearing and domineering nature later drove young Geli to take her own life.

The Great Depression, Blessing to Nazis

On the 29th October 1929, in the United States, events that could bring Hitler's peaceful times to an abrupt end happening. The U.S had taken over the struggling German economy, and the currency had recovered its value, but on that date , the Wall Street market in New York was wiped out, bringing all of the world into The Great Depression.

To Adolf Hitler, this was his signal that the time was coming to the next phase of his Nazi party's ascendance to power.

The Great Depression meant that banks collapsed across Germany and people were laid off and their savings disappeared, Germany's economy sank and hunger was a common occurrence. Inflation followed and a currency that was stabilised became useless paper. The Nazi party profited from people's fear of uncertainty, anger, as well as anger, feeding it, and promising promises, promises that the desperate people swarmed to.

1930 Elections

"What is the right of these individuals to have to ask for a portion of the property, or even to participate in the administration of property? ?... The person who takes on obligation to produce also grants workers a means to earn a living. The most successful industrialists of our time aren't interested in gaining wealth or living comfortably and most importantly, they are concerned by their power and responsibility. They've risen to the top of their field by their own capabilities and this proof of their capabilities which is only demonstrated by people of higher status has given them the ability to lead."

- Adolf Hitler

In the month of March in 1930 Heinrich Bruening became Chancellor of Germany. He was a target of opposition, but at the end of July 1930, he persuaded the president Hindenburg to dissolve the Reichstag and elections were scheduledto be held on September 14th.

Joseph Goebbels was the Nazi organizer of the events. He was given the job of organizing the events. He was a fervent worker by traversing the country and arranging meetings. Hitler delivered speeches at these scheduled meetings, and, as always, he impressed the crowds , particularly with his pledges. Employment for all, equality... take down the Treaty of Versailles and to eliminate all the people accountable for Germany's problems including, but not least Jews, Marxists along with the Jews.

Elections day came on September 14, 1930. After many years of struggle and promises, it was time to vote. was finally here. In the year 1938, Germans took to the ballot box, and the results resulted in an astonishing victory for Hitler. The Nazi party was granted an impressive 107 seats within the Reichstag. In the span of a few hours the Nazi party emerged from the shadows to become the second-largest political party within Germany.

Hitler is running for president of Germany

Things were beginning to look up the future of Adolf Hitler and his Nazi party. German industrialists were betting on him. His publication Mein Kampf was doing well and the world was taking note. He was contacted by numerous requests for interviews.

It was the German General Staff was also in support of Hitler, since Hitler had made a promise to expand the troops that was reduced to 100,000 soldiers following World War I defeat. There was one thing that stood against Hitler from the position he coveted- - the former president Paul von Hindenburg.

And then, amid the promise of power there was a dark cloud on Hitler; Geli, his niece and lover , committed suicide following a heated dispute. Hitler was a domineering, strict man who was averse to being corrected. Geli had an individuality and the constant surveillance was too much. So, in 1931, she committed suicide. This was a serious hit to Hitler but not a hindrance since he had already decided his intention to run for the presidency from Germany. Germany republic. His opponent was World War I Field marshal and the current President, aged 84, Paul Von Hindenburg.

The Great Depression had caused great suffering, and the German people were desperate and longing for relief. The Depression was now two years long. It was the hungry and starving population that Hitler turned his attention, again and again, promising jobs and retribution for the crimes was known as the November criminals. In the end, the Treaty of Versailles was another card he played a number of times and he wasn't done as the people begged for some relief. The present government appeared impervious and undecisive, because in 1932, elections were scheduled that were scheduled for the following year. However, the President at the time believed that he was too old for another run.

Hindenburg later opted to runfor office, however his strategies for campaigning stood in stark contrast to Hitler's loud, rowdy, and loud tactics. Joseph Goebbels, the Nazi party's organizer, once more was able to unite the people behind Hitler in support of Hitler and the Nazi party. Promises were made. Posters were put up and pamphlets made. Hitler was not left outand he delivered speeches after speeches promising food, work and security.

Hindenburg was a man who relied on his fame and image, and, save for some radio broadcasts did not put in the same effort as his competitors.

On the 13th of March, 1932, Germans were able to vote. The results- Hitler garnered 11,339,446) or 30% against

Hindenburg's 18,651,497 votes or 49%, of the total.

The run-off was needed because Hindenburg although leading was unable to win the majority. The run-off was planned for the 10th of April. Instead of lamenting in the sand, Hitler doubled his efforts and traveled across the country in an aircraft, rumbling his mouth awry in the exact same manner, promising food, work and the end of the shambles of a republic.

the president Hindenburg was silent. He did win. The 10th of April 1932 was an unseasonably rainy Sunday however it wasn't a triumphant storm for the Nazis. Hitler had been defeated. He lost the elections but not his popularity.

Spies, back stabbings, and Betrayals

"In all, in general, main goal of this cleansing process is to bring back an unnatural and sound equilibrium, and secondly take away from national positions of official importance those aspects to which it is not possible to entrust the survival of Germany or demise. Because it is not likely to be possible to avoid, over the coming years the need to ensure that certain procedures, which should not be disclosed to the the world, due to the most important national interest will remain in the shadows. This is only possible through the internal consistency of the administrative institutions involved."

- Adolf Hitler

Then there was Kurt Von Schleicher, an army officer whose goals were similar to Hitler's. The man who was scheming met Hitler the 8th of May, 1932 and offered Hitler Nazi chief a strategy. let the president dismantle the Reichstag and call for fresh elections. The cherry on top was having the Chancellor Bruening dismissed. All Hitler required to do was to pledge the support of Schleicher to which was what he did.

Schleicher was working on the former president. On the 30th May 1932 the Chancellor Bruening was the last person who had the respect of the masses, quit. Hitler was engaged in his own planning for the chancellor's job was to be announced in January of 1933.

A sequence of events was to propel Hitler into the coveted the Chancellorship, having lost the presidential election to Hindenburg.

Schleicher mentioned a man named Franz von Papen the Chancellor. In the meantime, the streets were becoming the scene of brawls for Nazi supporters as well as Communists. There was violence and bloodshed.

On the 17th of July, 19 people were killed and no more than 250 were injured when Nazis attacked the Communist region close to Hamburg. The following day, it was "Bloody Sunday."

In the end the Chancellor Papen announced the martial law of Berlin and was also appointed to the states of Prussia as the Reich Commissioner. For Hitler this man was a major obstruction.

Schleicher kept his word, and the Reichstag was disbanded and elections scheduled for the month of July, 1932. The Nazis ran their campaign with fervor and by July 31, 1932, voting was conducted. The Nazi party was victorious with 37% of the votes cast . They now had an impressive 230 seats in Reichstag. Hitler became the head of Germany's most powerful faction of Germany. This was the reason that he made his way to Schleicher on August 5, seeking to be appointed Chancellor. It took Schleicher eight days to give Hitler a reply- President Hindenburg had refused. Hitler was furiousand, since he held the majority in the house The Reichstag under the leadership of Hermann Goring gave a no confidence vote to the Papen government on the 12th of September.

Unfortunately, Papen as Chancellor had disbanded the Reichstagand scheduled new elections - yet again. The election of November 6th will be a time when the Nazi party losing some of its momentum with the loss of two million votes.

It was evident that the government wasn't doing well as well because the public were losing faith in it due to its indecisiveness. On November 17, Papen resigned as Chancellor of Germany.

Hitler continued to hold the Chancellorship. Now Hitler had the support of the nation's industrialists, powerful bankers and businessmen. They met with the President Hindenburg and requested that he nominate Hitler as the Chancellor. Hindenburg was hesitant, however, and demanded Paul Von Papen and Schleicher.

The two men sat down with the president, and both offered different suggestions on the best way to manage the government that is in disarray. The idea of Papen was to be chancellor once more and in order to bring his Reichstag into a close, eliminate any political party and alter the constitution. Schleicher sought the post of Chancellor.

.President Hindenburg sided with Papen to the displeasure Schleicher.

Unfortunately for Papen his army was with Hitler in addition, Hitler stood behind Schleicher as per their May agreement. Papen struggled to make a decision despite all the criticism and threats coming from Hitler who was still looking at the post of Chancellor.

Papen realizing the futility of the entire endeavor, contacted Hindenburg who was left with no choice other than to concede to Schleicher. So on the 2nd of December 1932 Kurt von Schleicher became the Chancellor of Germany.

On May 8 , 1932, Schleicher has met with Hitler to discuss a plan for how best to be able to take over the government but at the same time making sure that their interests are at the forefront. Schleicher had achieved what he set out to achieve, but it was exactly what that Hitler desired. The elections of July had given Hitler the largest number of votes in the Reichstag and he utilized that power to call the Chancellorship. Schleicher was the new Chancellor, however Hitler held the reins.

It was these reins that Schleicher decided to acquire to himself when he set out to dismantle his Nazi group from the inside. Hitler was aware of the plot through PapenHe was bitter over what he believed was an act of betrayal from Schleicher.

The two Hitler and Papen were able to come together to bring down Schleicher. The chancellor of the day did not do very well in a system which had come to an end. In addition even more, the same industrialists businessmen, and bankers who had previously contacted the previous president had approached him again. they were still convinced that Hitler would be the most suitable chancellor of Germany.

A Dream Fulfilled

Schleicher was quick to Hindenburg and suggested that he declare an emergency state and dissolve the Reichstag in a second time to suspend elections. Hindenburg refused. After the news spread about Schleicher's proposal his wrath was clearThen, on January 28, 1933 He demanded Hindenburg to dissolve the Reichstag. Hindenburg still refused. And Schleicher resigned.

Hindenburg was subject to so much pressure from all directions to make the necessary decisionthat only one person was worthy of the title of the Chancellor of Germany and then the former president gave in to pressureand on January 30th, 1933, he announced Adolf Hitler the new Chancellor of Germany.

Adolf Hitler had done it. From being homeless in Vienna and becoming a member of a shady party, he is now the new Chancellor of Germany and Papen was his Vice-Chancellor. A empathetic Hitler was greeted by thousands of supporters after the Chancellorship was announced. He repeated his promises to the masses and promised to bring Germany back into the spotlightand he achieved this five years later, when he plunged the nation into a war that was much more disastrous than the one in World War I. The whole thing was well-written by the late Erich Ludendorff.

The former General Erich Ludendorff had been a proponent of Hitler during the unsuccessful Beer Hall Putsch in 1923. However, he now hated Hitler and was not hesitant in sending the president Hindenburg the message he had sent to Hindenburg about Hitler.

"By appointing Hitler as Chancellor of the Reich you've handed over our Germany Fatherland for one of the most powerful demagogues in history. I am predicting that this evil person is going to plunge the Reich into the depths of hell and inflict a plethora of misery upon our people. The generations to come will be cursed in the tomb for this deed Ludendorff said.

This Law Concerns the Jews

"Those who were responsible for this calamity included the very same Jewish political parties that currently complain that their supporters are denied access to be elected officials, and with the same reason, as they are not of any use in these positions but are able to cause irreparable damage ..."

- Adolf Hitler

Chancellor Hitler has now decided to wipe out all opposition, both political or otherwise, through the A.S and gaining complete control over the Reichstag after having ensured that his party did not face opposition.

In the following days, he requested that the president Hinddenburg sign an act that gave his party the absolute power to identify and prosecute- even any person deemed as an imminent threat. The top of the list was the Jews.

In 1935, the following law were read by Reichstag president Hermann Goring concerning the Jews.

Reich Citizenship Law of September 15 in 1935.

I. 1. A subject of the state is a person that belongs to the union of protection that is the German Reich and is therefore bound by a particular obligation to the Reich.

2. The right to be a subject is gained according to the provisions in the Reich and State Law of Citizenship.

II. 1. An individual who is a citizen of Reich is a subject who is German or blood related to him and who, by his actions, proves that he's both eager and qualified for service to the German people and the Reich with a commitment to the Reich.

The Law for the Protection of German Blood

And German Honor, on September 15 and German Honor, September 15

Incredibly convinced that the pureness in German blood is vital for the continued existence of the German people, and enthused by the unwavering determination to secure for the long-term future of the German nation The Reichstag approved unanimously the law below, and it is issued herewith:

I. 1. Weddings that are between Jews and people of German or blood related to them are not permitted. Marriages that violate this law are invalid, even in the interest to avoid this law, they were made in another country. 2. An annulment proceeding can begin only with the help of the Public Prosecutor.

II. Sexual relations between Jews and citizens of German or blood related to them are prohibited.

III. Jews are not permitted to employ women of German or other blood relatives under 45 years old to serve as domestic helpers.

IV. 1. Jews are not allowed to fly the Reich as well as the national flag, as well as the colors of their nation. 2. On the other hand , they are allowed to display Jewish colors. The use of the right to display is protected by the state.

V. 1. Any person who violates to the provisions in Section I will be punished by hard labor. 2. Any person who violates to the provisions under Section II will be punished by imprisonment or hard work. 3. Anyone who is in violation to the requirements in Sections III and IV can be punished with a sentence of imprisonment for up to one year, and with a fine and/or with one or more of the punishments listed.

VI. VI. Reich Minister of Interior, with the deputy Fuhrer as well as the Reich Minister of Justice will issue the administrative and legal regulations for the enforcement and amendment of this law.

VII. The law will take effect upon the day following the promulgation of Section III will not be effective until January 1, 1936.

After Adolph Hitler made it to the top of the ladder and was appointed Chancellor of Germany Numerous things happened in quick time that culminated in the defeat of Germany in World War II and his suicide alongside his partner Eva Braun.

Post of Chancellor Not Enough

In 1933, Germany had the appointment of a new Chancellor, Adolf Hitler. Following his failed attempt to control the government with force ten years prior in November 1923 Hitler had appealed to the masses through his ability to persuade as well as Nazi party Joseph Goebbels, the propaganda minister, who was renowned for his campaign tactics. Their efforts helped the previously unpopular party gain power and, ultimately, resulted in Hitler in the position of being the President of Germany on January 30, 1933. So far, so good because he was able to rise to the top of the heap by ensuring he complied by the rules, which was, taking part in the elections through campaigning. However, that was soon to be over.

Hitler was a snob to his republican administration. With the support of his party , he determined to alter the laws to stamp any opposition to his plans that he had previously declared - and making all those accountable for the humiliation of Germany during the Great War pay dearly. The top of the list was the Jews But he needed to take another step before he could begin to pursue his agenda. It was a matter of the law. With the power of Chancellor, and he persuaded the President Hindenburg that he should call fresh elections- yet again.

President Hindenburg could have named Hitler as Chancellor in order to take the former president off his back however, the newly named Chancellor couldn't wait to be sworn into office. Hitler was already insisting that new elections be held as quickly as possible. His goals were to ensure that his party was in most of the seats in the Reichstag and consequently making it easier for him to make laws that were not opposed.

Hitler was always proud of himself as an enthusiastic German nationalist since his early age. The German loss in the Great War had left a bitter taste in his mouth. He always believed that it was the Jews for the many problems which confronted Germany including the loss of territories, the Armistice agreements, to the Treaty of Versailles- but the current administration and various political parties were an obstacle to his plans to win back German territories and, consequently, her glory gone. Now, with the Chancellorship, and the support of the people He revealed his real intentions before his German General Staff. He informed them that they would arm the army again and that conscription would be reinstated in the beginning in getting his country back into the spotlight.

Behind him was the powerful Nazi party of the Reichstag and in the streets were his storm troopers - they were the A.S and S.S, a brutal group made up of World War I soldiers who were known to Hitler and had joined to the Nazi political party, and are basing their lives on its strength and influence, as could be proven by the many inhumane acts they would unleash on those they believed to be anti-Nazi.

On February 24 on the 24th of February in Berlin they were able to raid Communist headquarters, and on the 27th February The Reichstag building was set ablaze. While the specifics of who or what burned the building aren't clear and it is believed that the Nazi party was suspected even though a communist, 24 -year aged Marinus van der Lubbe, who was 24 years old, was arrested for arson. This was a stroke luck for Hitlerand he was now able to have an acceptable and legitimate reason to eliminate the communistsand opposing parties in Germany. On February 28, 1938 the Emergency Decree was signed by the President Hindenburg on the orders of Hitler[4]. This decree gave Hitler as well as the Nazi party complete power. it was stated that

As per article 48(2)... ...following is declared as a measure of defense against acts of violence by communists that could endanger the security of the state:

...Therefore there are restrictions on individual liberty, the freedom of expression, which includes freedom of expression as well as the right to assembly and association, as well as violations of privacy in telephone, postal, and telephone communications and warrants for house searches, confiscation orders and restrictions on property are all permissible, even in excess of the legal limit stipulated.

The decree comes into force as of the date of the announcement.

Berlin 28th February 1933

The interpretation of this order in the Nazi party's perspective was the swift removal of Communists on the street, and even private residences with the help of Nazi S.A as well as the S.S. The storm troopers profited from the situation and arrested Social Democrats and liberals. The decree was a simple one that made it illegal for other political group to campaign or hold meetings, or even to publish anything remotely classified as "anti-Nazi".

The elections which President Hindenburg had requested at the request from Chancellor Hitler were set for the 5th day of March 1933. After their extensive campaigning and the dismantling on other parties as well as anti-Nazi publications, Nazis believed they would winhowever it wasn't to be. Elections were held on the same day as they were scheduled to take place however, the Nazis didn't get the two-thirds majority they required, and ended at only 44% of votes. The weeding had to be completed, with a ruthless. The goal of the party was to turn Hitler the dictator, legally.

A Dictator who is legally-approved

"Whenever I advocate in support of people like the German peasant, it's to protect the Volk. I do not have an ancestral manor nor estate... It is my belief that I am convinced that I am the only stateman around the globe who doesn't have an account in a bank. I do not hold any stock or shares in any company. I have never received or pay dividends."

- Adolf Hitler

The subsequent crackdowns were brutal. Government offices were sacked under the pretense of looking for "conspirators" but in reality office workers were exiled and replaced by the Nazis and their choice.

The massive arrests that were carried out, and the prisoners were treated in brutal ways - an early indication of the conditions that would be seen in the notorious concentration camps. In the days before the establishment of these camps, the old barracks for the army and abandoned manufacturing facilities were used for prisons.

On the 15th of March, 1933 Hitler as well as Goring held the cabinet meeting to discuss ways to convince the Reichstag to approve the Enabling Act. This law would grant Hitler the power to create any law he deemed needed, and also only controlling the budget, and approve any agreements that were signed with other governments.

There was a method to adopting the Act actually- the emergency decree which President Hindenburg signed granting the Nazi party the authority to search, stop and arrest any person suspected of being in opposition to Hitler or the Nazis.

On the 23rd of March The Reichstag where the Nazi party had secured just 44% of votes in the 5th March elections took place in Berlin to debate the passing of Nazi's Enabling Act. Officially this is the "Law to Removing the discontent from the The People as well as the Reich."

Before the vote, Hitler made a speech. He claimed the powers Hitler was looking for were to carry out crucially essential measures ...'

He reiterated the pledges were made repeatedly in the past, beginning in his early yearsending unemployment and a promotion of peace between the victorious Allies from World War I... However, only should the Reichstag approved the Enabling Act. The bill needed a two-thirds majority vote for. In the midst of the Reichstag building, there were troopers dressed in brown uniforms, and Swastika armbands. The moment for a decision was come and gone.

Voting was held and results were counted. 441 for, 84 against. Germany was not a democracy anymore with legal methods which he so passionately opposed the republic, it was made an dictator under his name Adolf Hitler.

The 1st April of 1933 was the day that the Jews would be experiencing the first glimpse of what was to followand a boycott of their products and companies that would grow and eventually lead to their death in the millions, an act of violence which would be a shock to the world.

Night of the Long Knives

In the days when Nazi was nothing more than a small movement in the beer halls back in 1919 an army informer been to the area in order to report back to his superiors and ended up staying as a memberand later as the leader. With just 7 people, the organization would expand, however, not without the assistance of one World War I combat officer known as Ernst Rohm who would become the Chief of Staff. Rohm would construct unstoppable army brutal storm troopers, referred to in the form of Sturmabteilung (A.S) and was the main force behind the rise of Hitler to power and would be there to support Hitler throughout his rise to power. In 1934, just 15 years after, Hitler was the Chancellor of Germany and this was not insignificantly because of the efforts of these raunchy and uncouth people who opened the way for him both metaphorically and literally. On the other hand the respected German General Staff had already pledged their support to the German General Staff. in the Treaty of Versailles had disarmed and diminished them to a force of 100,000 soldiers... However, Hitler had promised them rearmament and an increase... because they were still an entity to be taken seriously.

As Chancellor, and with increasing popularity, Hitler found himself in an impasse. Rohm was looking for storm troopers to be as the chief, was named"the" new German Army in order to replace General Staff German General Staff.

Because the traditional army was more admired by the general public as opposed to Rohm's untrained and rowdy men, it was easy to Hitler to choose, since the man he was becoming who was respected but also was determined to present a certain impression to German populace and other nations. With this mindset that in February 1934, Hitler was in conversation the S.A. S.A along with those who were the German Army leaders Rohm and Werner Von Blomberg respectively.

Hitler in unambiguous terms dispelled Rohm's plans to transform his soldiers into German Army- - and Rohm was in agreement. However, his signature did not express his actual feelings, which he expressed afterward in the presence of the troops, declaring Hitler "that crazy soldier... ...traitor ...' thoughts that didn't pass by Hitler's ears.

The SS (Schutzstaffel) were an elite group that was specially selected and commanded by Heinrich Himmler, and were personal loyal towards Adolf Hitler.

Himmler believed that there was a benefit in the distinctions in the two camps - Hitler and Rohmand made smart use of it by constantly depicting Rohm as a threat to Hitler's plans. In the wake of Rohm's fall, much could be gained and Himmler was with his second in command Reinhard

Heydrich, as well as an additional Nazi, Herman Goring, each of them with the intention to gain.

On June 4, Hitler met with Rohm to discuss ways to get things in order. it was apparent that this happened that it was a success. Rohm announced two days later that he was going on vacation, along with all of S.A. Hitler could breatheand relax, but things turned out to be the worse. Vice-Chancellor Papen claimed the possibility that Rohm was planning the beginning of a Second Revolution. On the 21st of June, Hitler met with President Hindenburg and General Blomberg of the General Staff. President Hindenburg did not shy away from his words. If Hitler didn't take action regarding the S.A potential threat could put an end to his Nazi rule by declaring martial laws and permitting Germany take over. German Army take over.

Tensions continued to grow because Hitler was naturally reluctant to take a stand against someone who had been a force for good. However, Himmler along with Goring were not letting up to spread rumors about potential putsch (overthrow).

A sequence of events in the coming days would lead to the purification of the S.A during what would later be known as the 'Night of Long Knives', which occurred on the 29th June 1934. Rohm and others who were considered to be a threat members of the Nazi party were detained and executed. The Nazi party had gone through the purge, losing many loyalists who joined Hitler alongside him when his rise to the top of the ladder.

Hitler is Fuhrer

On the 2nd of August 1934 The president Paul Von Hindenburg died and within the hours following his death the following law that was backdated to the 1st of August, was made public by the Reichstag [5, which was at the time the Nazi Reichstag:

The Reich Government has enacted the following law, which is now published.

Section 1. The post as Reich President would be combined with the office of Reich Chancellor. The authority currently held by

Reich President will be transferred to the Reich President will be handed over into Adolf Hitler, the Fuhrer as well as the Reich Chancellor Adolf Hitler. He will pick his deputy.

Section 2. The law takes effect at the time of the demise of Reich President of Hindenburg.

In the wake of news of the Fuhrer's new law that was announced, all members of the German Officer Corps and every soldier of the German Army took an allegiance oath:

"I swear to God this sacred swearing: I will give complete respect towards Adolf Hitler, the Fuhrer of the German Reich and people, the Supreme Commandant of the Armed Forces, and will be a fervent soldier to take my life anytime in order to fulfill this swearing."

On August 20, the swearing oaths of loyalty for every public official throughout Germany were introduced. They were required:

"I swear to remain loyal and faithful toward Adolf Hitler, the Fuhrer of the German Reich and to the German people. follow the law and carry out my official obligations with integrity I ask for help from God."

Tearing up the Treaty

"The Treaty of Versailles and the Treaty of St Germain are maintained in the form of Bolshevism within Germany. "The Peace Treaty and Bolshevism are two heads of one beast. We must decapitate both."

- Adolf Hitler

On March 15 1935 Hitler declared a key decision that the German General Staff- Germany to re-arm without regard to of the reality that he was in violation of the Treaty of Versailles.

Joseph Goebbels helped Hitler to write the proclamations to be made public to the populace and, the next day, which was a Saturday, Hitler delivered the proclamations to the Generals as well as the cabinet. He received their consent. The proclamations were later made public by Goebbels and then announced in a press conference and the crowds were glued to their seats. They waited for the Allies' (Britain and France) reaction.

The Allies didn't do anything. It was an unwise gamble for Hitler and he interpreted the Allies inaction as an acceptance. In the end, Versailles Treaty suffered the first tear.

He was still an official and on May 21 He spoke in a gentle tone to the world that could be a bit frightened by stating that what Germany wanted was peace. Then he added that Germany would abide by the Treaty which he was set to break and his intention was to be the leader of Germany in the promotion of European peace.

The Rhineland comprised cities such as Cologne, Dusseldorf, Bonn as well as all the land that was west of Rhine River that extended to the French border. In the early morning of March 7th , 1936 The German army entered the Rhineland. Hitler had fulfilled his threats. It was clear that the Treaty of Versailles had another tear-filled blame Hitler and it was not be the last.

In fact, he wanted the world to be aware of the fact that on the same day that the army crossed the bridges that crossed the Rhine the German Foreign Minister Constantin Von Neurath met representatives of the

French, British and Italian ambassadorsand handed the ambassadors a note stating that Germany had taken back "the demilitarized zone" of the Rhineland'.

The Berlin Olympics

1936 Olympic Games were held in Nazi Germany. They were organized by the International Olympic Committee had awarded Germany the Games in May 1931. However, the whole concept did not impress Hitlerwho was then Fuhrer (Supreme leader) Joseph Goebbels, however, was aware of the potential for abuse the Games had, and that it would be a good chance for the world to know how superior Germany was. Another thing Hitler was keen to prove was his assertion about the supremacy and power of the "Aryan Race" over the rest of the races.

The ceremony of opening was held on August 1 in 1936. Fifty one countries were present.

The extreme zeal and close-to-worship reverence that the Games hosts will display to their leader will make the other world leaders pay attention to this brand new German Fuhrer.

Hitler Hears a hankering for War

"Truly the earth is a trophy cup to the hardworking man. It is a righteous thing to serve natural selection. Whoever does not have the power to secure his Lebensraum within this universe, and, if required to expand it is not worthy of the basic necessities of existence. He should step back and let more powerful people overtake him."

- Adolf Hitler

Adolf Hitler had just two main goals. His goal was the expansion of Germany (Lebensraum) and retribution on his fellow Jews for their part in the defeat for Germany during the Great War of 1914-1918. This was the main reason that drove his unending pursuit of power, and now that he was in the position, he was the Fuhrer who had been christened so. It was the Nazi Reichstag had approved a law that merged the power of the president and those of the

Chancellor shortly after the demise of the president Paul von Hindenburg.

In 1935 Hitler reinstated conscription in the military in order to build the German Army. In the following calendar year German troops had crossed across the Rhine Bridge and occupied the Rhineland in a move that was completely in violation of Versailles Treaty. The world was aware of it, however, they did nothing.

On November 5 in 1937 Hitler laid out his plan to obtain Lebensraum in Germany. Hitler had spoken to the Polish ambassador earlier that day and gave his assurance via an agreement signed by Poland that the country's right to territorial sovereignty would be honored. However, his grand plans were being challenged by his Army Generals. There was a need to take action.

The Commander of the Armed Forces

It was true that the German Army was admired, however, its generals did not possess the same fervor as Hitlerparticularly regarding what he called "acquiring more land to people of the German people. They viewed his actions as unnecessary and risky and warned him as many times when he crossed into Rhineland in 1936. Field Marshal Werner von Blomberg was the Chief of Staff for the German Armed Forces, while General Werner von Fritsch was the Chief of Staff for the Army.

Since his earliest days, Adolf Hitler hated being corrected or questioned. This was a characteristic that he grew up with. As his position as the Fuhrer of Germany was a man who demanded complete respect from people like Blomberg as well as Fritsch. But it was evident that those men, if not controlled, could be an obstacle to Hitler's plans He therefore arranged for their demise and again, Hermann Goring and Heinrich Himmler who were the two men who worked tirelessly to bring down Ernst Rohm, set to work. Blomberg was dismissed in January 1938 after he had married an ex-prostitute (he was able to go ahead with the wedding following being urged by Goring and had advised Hitler). Fritsch was on the other hand was accused of homosexuality. Hitler placed him on permanent leave after he refused to quit. The gap between the two men left had to be filledand on February 4, 1938 Hitler called a Cabinet meeting. the Cabinet and a decree that reads that 'from now on, I will personally take over the overall command of the Armed Forces' was promulgated.

A homeless man leaves Vienna in 1913.

A Leader Resurfaces in 1938

"Bolshevism is a threat to not just private property, but also private initiative and the willingness to take the responsibility. It hasn't been able to help millions of humans from hunger in Russia which is the largest Agrarian state in the entire world. It is impossible to bring such a disaster to Germany since it is the case that at the end of the day it is the case that there are a lot of people in Russia the city population is 10 to each 90 rural dwellers however, in Germany for just 25 farmers There are 75 urban residents. Both the National Socialists and Bolshevists each believe they're worlds apart from one another, and that their differences cannot be reconciled. Beyond that it was the case that thousands of our citizens murdered and wounded in the battle against Bolshevism. If Russia is a fan of Bolshevism it's not our concern However, should Bolshevism extends its nets to Germany and we are able to combat it with all our might."

On March 12 in 1938, German soldiers in tanks entered Germany-Austria. Just a few years ago, German troops had marched into Rhinelandbut France and Britain did nothing. Then, Hitler had roared into Austriabut they had did absolutely nothing.

Violence against Jews broke out in Vienna after the Nazis had entered the city. Every single person was targetedfrom the looting of stores to homes as well as the destruction of their religious sites of worship, and even imprisonment without cause.

Heinrich Himmler set up the first concentration camp in Mauthausen close to Linz. Nearly 120,000 people ended dying in the camp's quarry of granite or killed for trying to escape.

Austria was captured without one shot fired. The next target for Hitler would be Sudetenland, Czechoslovakia.

"Handed Sudetenland to a Plate'

The next nation to have Hitler's military interests was Czechoslovakiaand was planned for an attack on October after having joined Austria on the 12th of March.

The world was starting to feel anxious and, on the 15 September 1938, Hitler received a visit from Neville Chamberlain, the British Prime Minister. His task is to persuade Hitler not to strike Czechoslovakia and, despite the fact that the German Fuhrer was begging for war but the other Germans as well as the rest of the world were less enthusiastic and didn't have the same enthusiasm and enthusiasm as he did.

The negotiations took place over time, and on the 30th of September, during the meeting at Munich with Hitler, Chamberlain, Mussolini and Edouard Daladier (the French Prime Minister) The Munich Agreement became a reality providing Hitler Sudetenland. The only thing he needed to do was promise not to strike the remainder of Czechoslovakia. The German Army took over the Sudetenland territory on the 1st of October 1938.

Everything Hitler desired, he receivedeasily and quickly. However, he was still aching for war, and most likely looked ahead to showing the people around the world that Germany wasn't the only one who lost World War I; he was challenging the world's other powers, mocking them, and seeking reasons for an all-out military assault and not the "I need thisokay, go for it' scenario unfolding; he was flying through Austria without a fight and was handed the Sudetenland "on a platter" according to his description of as the Munich Agreement.

Chapter 9: Path To Ruin

"I am aware, as are Duce, Duce, how difficult to make historical decisions, however I'm not sure if following my death, a successor is found using the force required by will...I believe it is the goodness of Providence that I was chosen to lead my nation in this conflict." -- Adolf Hitler to Benito Mussolini in one of his letters addressed to the Italian leader

A) Assassination Aims

In securing all power to Hitler, Hitler "won" a few foes including some who would have him killed. Hitler knew about this, which is why he asked Nazi members to form paramilitary groups that would act as a shield for him or other Nazi high-ranking officials. Many of the assassination attempts were planned through German citizens, since Jews or any other ethnic group could not even come close to the Fuhrer. In the 1920s, Hitler was practically obscure outside Bavaria as well as his SA could shield against any political foe within the region. He was a small person and was merely an angry person, therefore there isn't any evidence of assassination attempts against Hitler during this time. In the process of becoming an extremely influential people in the political world in Germany He had enemies in other political parties, but as well as the Nazi party in its own right. However, none were as radical or as a threat as Hitler and therefore, they were never any threat to his life. The situation was to change in 1932, when Hitler was elected the leader of the largest group in Germany. In the years following there were numerous attempts to take down Hitler however, the majority of which were discovered at time by SS leadership, so the Fuhrer was alive until the very end in World War II.

There were at least 42 unsuccessful attempts at assassinating Hitler between 1932 and the last attempt in July 1944. A few of these attempts were made by former combatants from the Freikorps (Beppo Romer, who was involved in multiple attempts) and the German carpenter (Johann Georg Elser) as well as the German diplomatic official (Erich Kordt) as well as an

German Jewish man (Helmut Hirsch), Polish officers, as well as a mentally challenged patient. The most dangerous attacks on Hitler's life were carried out by the officers from The German Army. The majority of German officers believed Hitler was bringing the nation to ruinand considered it their duty as a patriotic nation to kill Hitler as the Fuhrer and take over Germany to negotiate with the Allies regarding different terms. Although the Fuhrer granted them ranks and medals but these officers felt that they were deprived of their power and power, since the Fuhrer was deciding on the strategy of war instead of them. Maybe they could have accepted this if Hitler had had prior experience as an officer in the German Army However, they knew they were aware that Hitler was a dispatch runner, who was not a participant during World War I and most of all, didn't know anything regarding military strategies. Hitler's war plan resulted in many deaths in the Wehrmacht because many of his plans were not able to be sustained on the battlefield.

First attempt by army officers to murder Hitler by officers of the army was planned by army officers in September 1938, at the time Hitler had plans to attack Czechoslovakia. General Major Hans Oster and other officers planned to detain or shoot Hitler in the event that the latter attempted to invade Czechoslovakia. The plan was to take the power to take over Hitler with the Emperor who had been exiled Wilhelm II. Since it was the case that the Munich peace conference gave an offer of the Sudetenland to Germany the plan did not happen. However, a few officials were part of the future plans to thwart Hitler. The tide of war was shifting and the odds were in favor of the German Army and the plots became more frequent. In the meantime, Hitler already lost the Battle of Moscow and the Battle of Stalingrad due to his war plan and top officers conspired to overthrow and kill the Fuhrer. Hitler had planned to visit Ukraine to look over Kempf's Army Detachment Kempf, which means that this was the perfect time for generals such as Hubert Lanz, Hans Speidel as well as Hyazinth Graf Strachwitz besiege Hitler and his escort Fuhrer as well as his entourage tanks to detain or even murder Hitler as well as those who were the SS guards. Due to unknown reasons, the visit was postponed.

Another attempt took place on the 13th of March 1943 The day that Hitler went to his Army Group Center in Smolensk. Major Georg von Boeselager had planned to kill and intercept the Fuhrer (with assistance from other officers) as he traveled between the airfield and the station, however the massive number of SS soldiers guarded Hitler therefore he couldn't execute the plan. Henning of Tresckow, and Boeselager had planned to kill Hitler in the afternoon, but they abandoned the plan because Himmler was not with Hitler. Field Marshal Gunther von Kluge was aware the plot, but didn't wish to be involved in the plot. After the Fuhrer returned to his aircraft, Tresckow gave to an officer of Hitler's escort a bomb disguised as a liquor. The bomb was to explode upon the return flight, which was over Poland but the box was put in the hold of the aircraft and instead of popping it stopped freezing, and caused an ignition system to malfunction. Confronted with the failure of the attempt the soldier identified as Fabian von Schllabrendorff took off for Germany to retrieve the suitcase prior to it being discovered. There were other efforts by German soldiers to murder Hitler but none came similar to the plot of 20th July, that was also referred to as Operations Valkyrie. The central part in the story was played out by the Colonel Claus von Stauffenberg, a young German officer who participated during the war between Poland as well as that of the Soviet Union, and also in Northern Africa. With Major General Friedrich Olbricht and Major General Henning von Tresckow, he aimed to murder Hitler and then arrest the Nazi leaders, and disarm SS troops. The idea was to bring an explosive into the Wolf's Lair (Hitler's Hidden Command Center) in the hope of killing Hitler and to also mobilize his German Reserve Army to seize the power. General von Stauffenberg successfully introduced the suitcase into the Command Center. The attempt, however, failed to cause the death of the Fuhrer. There was a huge explosion but Hitler was able to survive and all the officers that conspired with him to murder were detained for high Treason (and eventually executed).

B) Territory Loss

For Germany the war ended following The Battle of Moscow and the Battle of Stalingrad. Hitler was able to lose a significant amount of his resources along the Eastern Front, including countless human victims. Many soldier's lives were lost in these battles on the Eastern front as well. The Fuhrer was able to replace these soldiers with civilians. In addition, many artillery guns and tanks were lost in the wars on that Eastern front. Germany could not meet the loss because industries in Germany could not provide the same number of guns, planes, tanks and rifles or machine guns. For the civilians most of them were too young or old which meant they weren't beneficial to Hitler. Given these conditions the Wehrmacht was forced to conduct an offensive war because they were no longer receiving assistance from the Luftwaffe and did not have the resources needed to conduct an entire offensive. They were forced to leave Russia,

Ukraine, and the Baltic states as they were unable to fight Soviet troops. Soviet troops.

But it was it was the German Army would stage a major final defense on its Eastern front during the Battle of Kursk. It was the largest tank battle in the history of warfare in the history of tanks, with Germany on one hand with half a million soldiers with 10000 mortars and guns, and 2700 tanks and about 2500 planes. In contrast, the Soviet Union was even better equipped, with 1.3 million soldiers and more than 20 thousand mortars and guns, approximately 3600 tanks, and around 2650 planes. Additionally they included half a million troops and 1500 tanks in reserves. Although it was true that the Russians beat the Germans in terms of men and more military equipment, losses were much greater for both sides. Russian side. The brand new Tiger tank that was used by the Germans proved extremely efficient in the battle, however, it was unable to be a major difference and the Soviets prevailed in the war, despite having to pay a huge price. The Wehrmacht didn't recover from the devastating blow that was the conflict at the

Eastern Front, as they could not replace all the destroyed personnel and armour. In the end they Nazis had to withdraw as well on other fronts in addition to that of the Eastern one. They had no longer been present within Northern Africa and they had to fight on Italian territory, while the Allies were moving toward Rome. Within the Soviet Union, the Russian troops were in the process of chasing down German troops, and were following them toward Germany through Ukraine as well as Poland, the Baltic States, and Poland.

Because the Allies were unable to advance towards Germany through Italy (because due to the Alps) and they needed to open their Western front. On June 6 of 1944, 1944 on June 6, 1944, the Allies arrived at Normandy in a brave attempt to advance toward Germany. An estimated 156 thousand British, American, and Canadian troops were landed at the shores of Normandy. The Nazis faced a strong resistance however, the allies prevailed , and gained the control of Normandy. Within a short time Normandy's beaches Normandy were inundated with over 326

000 soldiers, 100 000 tonnes of equipment, and over fifty thousand cars. As enemies surrounded these beaches from both the east, and from the West The German Army was forced to fight for their home, since they were being bombarded by the Allies were already bombarding German cities.

In the early days of the war against Soviet Russia, Nazi Germany controlled the majority of the continent of Europe. But, by the time it was over, the situation was drastically different. In the absence of manpower and armor and supplies, the Wehrmacht was unable to stand for much longer and, in the 11 months from to the Normandy Invasion, the war would end with the German Army loss.

C) The Last Days

In the final days of 1944 in the year 1944, the Soviet Army as well as the Allied forces were already moving toward Germany. In the absence of an enormous offensive against both sides, he decided to take on the Allied troops because it was his belief as if it was the Red Army was far stronger. On the 16th Dec 1944 Hitler declared the

Ardennes Offensive, a desperate effort to force back the Allies back. Its Reserve Army mobilized for this operation experienced a few brief victories, however, the Allies were able to fight back and continued to march into Germany. In the beginning of January 1945, a huge area of Germany was already in ruin and Hitler required more drastic measures. He did not want the German industry to be taken over by the Allies hands, and so he ordered the destruction all industrial structures across Germany. Albert Speer, who in the final years was the Minister for Armaments who was charged with the task, but he did not continue to perform the task in secret, ignoring Hitler's instructions. The passing of American President Roosevelt was a catalyst that gave Hitler the chance to negotiate an agreement to end the war between his allies, the US as well as Great Britain. But, it didn't happen because the allies did not want to engage in negotiations with Hitler.

There is a possibility that some high-ranking Nazi leaders have managed to escape Berlin (while Berlin was being bombed and attacked by Soviet forces) and then fled into

South America (via Italy). It appeared that the continent's countries were the perfect location to Nazi members to escape the law, knowing that the Allies did not show any mercy. There is also the possibility that Hitler was able to escape and flee towards South America, but most historians aren't convinced. In the final days of the conflict, Hitler was hiding in his bunker in Berlin in readiness for the inevitable. On the 20th of April 1945 Hitler gave his final public address in the gardens in the Reich Chancellery. Hitler made the final preparations to defend Berlin and placed an army group called the Army Group Vistula outside Berlin to stop from the Red Army advance and also included a small number of insufficiently equipped soldiers put under the control by Felix Steiner, the commander of the Waffen SS. On the 21st of April 1945 the Soviet Army had destroyed all defenses that was part of that of the German Army as well as in the process of preparing for a bombardment of Berlin. Two days later they completely covered the German capital, and then meticulously bombarded Berlin and advancing street by street, and destroying all German resistance.

Goebbels encouraged the citizens in Berlin in Berlin to fight for their town however, they could not stand up to The Red Army. In all of this, Goring was at Bertechsgaden in the Bavarian Alps away from the bombings in Berlin and awaiting his turn to take on the role of leader. Goring wrote a letter to the Fuhrer with arguments for why Goring should become the leader, since the Fuhrer was being surrounded by Berlin. He also set a date that he wanted to meet with his Fuhrer, Goring considering that should Hitler didn't respond the reason was that he was disabled. On April 28 Hitler found out his mistake. Himmler was emigrating from Berlin on the 20th of April and was contemplating surrender and negotiating in negotiations with Allies. The Fuhrer demanded to arrest Himmler and, in his personal will, he stripped Goring of all of his positions in the government. Goring was soon informed of the execution of Mussolini, and was stronger determined to avoid being captured at any cost. The Grand Admiral Karl Donitz was appointed the head of the state, and Joseph Goebbels was named chancellor.

www.ingramcontent.com/pod-product-compliance
Lightning Source LLC
Chambersburg PA
CBHW050359120526
44590CB00015B/1757